GriefWork for Teens

Healing from Loss

Reproducible
Interactive
& Educational
Handouts

by Ester R. A. Leutenberg & Fran Zamore, MSW, ACSW

Illustrated by
Amy L. Brodsky, LISW-S

wholeperson
Stress & Wellness Publishers

Duluth, Minnesota

wholeperson
Stress & Wellness Publishers

101 West 2nd Street, Suite 203
Duluth, MN 55802

800-247-6789

Books@WholePerson.com
WholePerson.com

GriefWork for Teens ~ Healing from Loss
Reproducible Interactive & Educational Handouts

Copyright ©2012 by Ester R. A. Leutenberg and Fran Zamore.
All rights reserved.

This book contains original reproducible activity handouts, exclusive with Whole Person Associates, and fully protected by copyrights. The original purchaser of this book is authorized to reproduce and use the handouts in this book for the generation of creative activity in a therapeutic, educational, and/or group setting. The reproducible handouts in this book may not be reprinted or resyndicated in whole or in part as a reproducible handout, book, or collection, or for any other purpose without the written permission of the publisher.

This publication is sold with the understanding that the publisher is not engaged in rendering psychological, medical, or other professional services.

Printed in the United States of America

10 9 8 7 6 5 4 3 2 1

Editorial Director: Carlene Sippola
Art Director: Joy Morgan Dey

Library of Congress Control Number: 2012936858
ISBN: 978-1-57025-262-4

DEDICATION

GriefWork for Teens ~ Healing from Loss
**is dedicated to the memory of
all of those whom we've loved and lost.**

OUR THANKS & GRATITUDE

**To our families for their support
with this book and in our lives.**

To the following whose input we truly appreciate:

Annette Damien, MS, PPS
Tanya Gamby, Ph.D.
Beth Jennings, CTEC
Jay Leutenberg
Michael Rhine, M.S., LMHC
Kari Weileder, MAT, LSC

**To Amy L. Brodsky, LISW-S, whose creative, thoughtful illustrations
give our words reality and added meaning.**

**To each other for friendship, support, encouragement,
tears and laughter throughout the years!**

— Ester & Fran

TABLE OF CONTENTS

Table of Contents 4–5

I For the Facilitator

About *GriefWork for Teens* — Healing from Loss 7–8
The Grief Experience 9
Definitions 10
Kinds of Losses 10
The Healing Pathway 11–12
Tasks of Healing from a Loss 13
Facilitation Tips 14–15
Taking Care of Yourself 16

II – 1 Let's Get Started

Introduction for the Facilitator 17
Permissions and Guidelines 19–20
Ribbon Activity 21–22
The Healing Pathway 23–24
The Healing Pathway (Poster) 25–26
Tasks of Healing from a Loss (for the participant) 27–28
Rights of Teens Experiencing Grief 29–30

II – 2 Getting in Touch

Introduction for the Facilitator 31
Teen GriefWork Emotions 33–34
The Emotions Salad Bowl 35–36
Serenity Prayer 37–38
Control 39–40
Fear 41–42
My Regrets 43–44
You're Not Alone 45–46
What to Do With My Memories? 47–48

II – 3 Telling Your Story

Introduction for the Facilitator 49
Memento Activity 51–52
What I Miss 53–54
Part of My Story is 55–56
When I Experienced the Loss of My Loved One 57–58

II – 4 Self-Care

Introduction for the Facilitator 59
Self-Care Domains 61–62
Are You Taking Care of Yourself? 63–64

TABLE OF CONTENTS

II – 4 Self-Care (Continued)

Counting My Blessings	65–66
Ways to Nourish Myself	67–68
Spontaneity and Impulsive Behavior	69–70
Accomplishments	71–72
Being the Best You Can Be	73–74
A Sacred Space	75–76
My Prayer	77–78
Need a Good Cry?	79–80
It Helps to Smile	81–82
Self-Talk	83–84

II – 5 Relationships

Introduction for the Facilitator	85
My Support Network	87–88
Support System	89–90
Relationships Change	91–92
Supportive Friends	93–94
They Mean Well	95–96
Why Do Friends Drop Away?	97–98
Notes to Family & Friends After a Loss	99–100

II – 6 A New Normal

Introduction for the Facilitator	101
Healing	103–104
What has Changed in My Life?	105–106
Coping with Special Days and Holidays	107–108
Holidays and Special Events	109–110
Empty House	111–112
✤ How Can I Honor _____ ?	113–114
I Loved Just the Way _____ Was, However	115–116
Looking Towards the Future	117–118
Moving Forward	119–120
Affirmations	121–122
I Have Choices	123–124

III – Resources 125–126

✤ *Specifically Related to Death*

SECTION I

For the Facilitator

This section is specifically designed as background information. We encourage you to read the material before using this book.

We have provided information to help with understanding of the grieving process as well as suggestions for using the book. You will also find ideas for individual and group facilitation.

About *GriefWork for Teens*

We intend to provide school counselors, therapists and other mental health professionals with resources that will elevate conversations about loss and aid in the grieving process. Through our work with teens who are grieving, and drawing from our personal experiences, we have become fully aware of the complexities associated with grieving. We live in a society where people are expected to 'get-over' their loss quickly and we understand this is not realistic. We know there are many ways that teens grieve and we support one's right to grieve in an individual and unique fashion.

GriefWork for Teens is for facilitators to help grieving teens heal from their losses. Everyone experiences loss. We refer to the psychological process of coping with a significant loss as grief work. The range of behaviors, emotions and attitudes is huge. Throughout the book we use the terms *normalize* and *New Normal* to convey that everyone's grief has a unique expression and is that particular teen's 'normal.'

The handouts in *GriefWork for Teens* will engage those who grieve any type of loss and encourage them to identify, internalize and/or verbalize personal feelings while working through the grieving process. The only page specific to death is *How Can I Honor* _____, pages 113 and 114.

GriefWork for Teens contains activity and educational handouts and journaling pages which can be used in individual counseling sessions, educational settings and support groups. We strongly suggest that before sharing the handouts in this book, you complete them yourself, remembering a loss you have experienced. By doing the activities you will better understand the value, and some of the likely reactions to the activity. It will also increase your comfort level and your confidence in using the handouts. It is possible and quite probable that you, as well as the teens you work with, will grow emotionally and spiritually while doing this important work.

Each interactive activity has comments and suggestions on the back explaining the purpose of the activity and at least one way to use it. Read them prior to using the handout to get the most out of each one and to give you a 'starter-idea.' Be creative in using this book. Although the handouts are written for use in groups, they may be adapted to use with individuals or as homework assignments.

(Continued on the next page)

About *GriefWork for Teens* (Continued)

The handouts are all reproducible, allowing the facilitator to keep the book intact. They can be adapted for a particular group by photocopying a handout, using white-out to eliminate what might not be appropriate for a particular group, and writing in your own words and using that as the master copy for that group. Photocopy as many as needed to distribute for direct teen use.

Look through the handouts and select one or more to use each session. Not all handouts will be appropriate for all participants; it is imperative to carefully select handouts for your particular group (or teen) based on the number of sessions you anticipate and the particular issues being presented to them. Encourage participants to use the activities that are applicable. Expect and accept that some will not be interested in filling out the handouts, but they may gain from the group discussion.

Use Codes for Confidentiality

Confidentiality is a term for any action that preserves the privacy of other people. Because teens completing the activities may be asked to journal about and explore their relationships, you will need to discuss confidentiality before you begin using the materials in this book. Maintaining confidentiality is important because it shows respect for others and allows participants to explore their feelings without hurting anyone's feelings or fearing gossip, harm or retribution.

In order to maintain confidentiality, explain to the participants that they need to assign a **name code for each person or each group of people** they write about as they complete the various activities. For example, a friend named Joey who enjoys going to hockey games might be titled JLHG (Joey Loves Hockey Games) for a particular exercise. In order to protect the identity of others, they should not use people's or groups' actual names or initials, just name codes.

The Grief Experience

One of the important aspects of grieving that has been largely overlooked is the relational aspect. Each person's grief is unique because he or she:

- Had a unique relationship with a deceased person (loving, ambivalent, challenging)
- Brings a unique personality and coping mechanism to the situation
- Has a particular world view which will impact how he or she enters the process
- Has ongoing relationships which may or may not be helpful
- Came to this particular loss with a unique history of dealing with earlier losses
- Has particular expectations about what dealing with the loss means and wonders how dealing with the loss "should" proceed
- Has misconceptions or preconceptions of dealing with death from the media
- Is dealing with death for the first time

The grieving process can occur in many types of losses; most of these pages are applicable to any type of loss. See asterisk on Table of Contents for the page that focuses on death only.

The grieving process is impacted by each teen's developmental stage and issues. A teen may experience profound grief over losses that adults in his/her life may think are trivial or fleeting. While not encouraging over-dramatization, which some teens are prone to, it is important to be accepting of each teen's unique emotional state.

We view the grieving experience as a long, winding path that curves back on itself, traverses hills and valleys, and has many obstacles. It is a path that is challenging to negotiate, time-consuming to travel along and may provide opportunities for personal and spiritual growth. Grieving is a part of the human experience. A teen attached to someone will mourn the loss of that relationship and miss that person's physical presence – even when loss is caused by moving, break-up, or loss of friendship – not necessarily death.

Definitions

LOSS refers to no longer having somebody or something, tangible or intangible.
GRIEF is the reaction to a loss. It is a universal response to any loss.
BEREAVEMENT refers to the experience of the loss of someone through death.
MOURNING refers to the expression of grief in culturally specific ways.

Kinds of Losses

Loss is a part of everyone's life at some point. Each person reacts to a loss in a personal way. As well as the emotional response, loss also has physical, intellectual, behavioral, social and philosophical dimensions. Response to loss is varied and is influenced by beliefs and practices.

Teens' losses, no matter what, are important and often devastating to them. They represent the disappearance of something or someone cherished.

Some examples of loss:
- Addiction
- Change in family structure
  (older sibling moving, baby entering family, step-family)
- Change of school
- Childhood
- Death
- Divorce
- Faith
- Friends moving away
- Home
- Innocence
- Moving away from friends
- Moving away to college
- Pet
- Physical health
- Plans, hopes and dreams
- Relationships
- Sense of safety/security
- Serious accident
- Suicide
- Treasured possessions

THE HEALING PATHWAY

The purpose of THE HEALING PATHWAY is to provide a framework and a common language for talking about the grieving experience without timelines. As teens go through the process of grieving a loss, they will likely go through this process and experience:

    1. Shock   2. Disorganization   3. Reorganization

We view the process as recursive. As the shock of the loss wears off and teens start to experience their feelings fully and learn to manage them, they will begin to reorganize their lives. As this healing occurs, they will have times when they find themselves dealing again with very primitive feelings and think they are back at the beginning of the process. We liken this to a path that keeps curving back on itself. Holidays, birthdays and other special occasions can flip the grieving person back; these setbacks will not be as intense nor will they last as long as previous setbacks. Perhaps they will also be less surprising, therefore lessening the feeling of being blindsided.

Teens who have an ill loved one may experience anticipatory grief and anticipatory mourning as their loved one's health declines. Many people are surprised when this anticipatory work does not inoculate them against the pain of the loss. We know that it does not! Anticipatory grief may mitigate the intensity and duration of the shock of the loss, but will not reduce the need for learning how to manage.

In THE HEALING PATHWAY we explain that the first experience is one of *shock*. The numbness that is associated with this can be very misleading; often others think that the teen is not grieving. In addition to numbness, shock is often characterized by disbelief that the loss actually occurred, and searching behavior (looking for the loved one in crowds or familiar places) is quite common.

Shock can last for a few days or longer, often depending on the circumstances. Teens who are coping with a sudden, tragic loss will often be in *shock* for a long time.

Shock gradually wears off and as that is happening, and reality sinks in, teens move to a phase we call *disorganization*. This is 'the pits.' It is the phase that takes the longest to emerge from and is the place which everyone who grieves returns to time and time again, with diminishing intensity and duration. *Disorganization* is characterized by feeling the full impact of the loss. Yearning, missing, sadness, heavy-heartedness are all common. Teens also experience relief, fear of life without the missing person, and/or anger. The important work during this phase of THE HEALING PATHWAY is to ultimately feel the wide array of emotions.

(Continued on the next page)

THE HEALING PATHWAY *(Continued)*

It is also during *disorganization* that teens have difficulty concentrating which may contribute to academic challenges. Accidents are likely to happen during this phase as reflexes are also diminished and there is often an increase in risky behavior. Other common physical symptoms of *disorganization* include interrupted sleep patterns, appetite changes and general lethargy. The good news is that this is not a permanent state. *Disorganization* leads to the next phase, *reorganization*. The lines between these two phases are fluid, and there is a great deal of going back and forth.

Reorganization is characterized by emerging from the fog of *disorganization*. This is when some teens are able to consciously decide that they will take the experience of loss and grieving and use it as impetus for their personal growth.

Active grieving will dissipate over time. Memories will remain. There will be times when something triggers a particular memory and the grieving teen may feel thrust back. It is important to keep in mind that these feelings are normal and will recur. One hopes that this going "back in time" will not last long. The teen grieving will have learned how to feel feelings, relish memories and move on. They continue to learn and grow as they recycle their experiences.

The purpose of THE HEALING PATHWAY is to help teens establish a *NEW NORMAL*. By *NEW NORMAL*, we are consciously referring to each individual's unique experience. It must be clearly understood that *NEW NORMAL* is not a static destination and is unique to each individual. Each teen has a unique way of being in the world. My *NEW NORMAL* will be **what is right for me**; your *NEW NORMAL* will be **what is right for you**. Developing a *NEW NORMAL* – a relatively comfortable way of living in one's current circumstances – is the goal.

As the teens travel along THE HEALING PATHWAY, we are supporting the work necessary to help them live with gratitude for what they had, live in the present with joy and focus on what lies ahead.

Tasks of Healing from a Loss
For the Facilitator

Four tasks are related to the work of grieving. Personal growth and healing are built on these tasks.

1. **Accepting the loss** is the starting point for the work of grieving. Accepting the loss refers not only to intellectual acceptance, it also refers to emotional recognition. Intellectual acceptance occurs as a person emerges from *shock*. Full emotional acceptance may take longer and occurs as the other tasks are being accomplished.

2. **Feeling the feelings** is counter-intuitive for most teens. They would rather deny feelings, push them aside, distract themselves and/or 'stuff' them instead of experiencing the full weight of any uncomfortable emotions. Experiencing feelings is imperative and is a primary task during *disorganization*. Not all teens will be able, or willing to express their feelings, and that is okay. It is helpful to be able to identify them. Some teens feel what they are feeling and do not need to emote. We must allow for differences in expressive styles and not insist that feelings be expressed in any particular way.

3. **Adjusting** relates to learning to live with the loss. Reorganizing one's life depends on the nature of the loss. For teenagers, this means being able to return to prior levels of functioning with schoolwork, friends, and in the context of their homelife. We associate this process with the stage of *reorganization* along THE HEALING PATHWAY.

4. **Moving forward** is when we notice that the grieving teen has been able to adjust in a way that allows for personal growth. Moving forward does not imply forgetting. It is a recognition of living life fully, being grateful for all we *do* have, with a genuine capacity for joy, in a newly constituted way and formulating a vision for the future. This coincides with the concept of NEW NORMAL.

Facilitation Tips

Facilitating groups is often challenging due to the complexities of different personalities and issues; therefore we are including basic information pertinent to educational and support groups, particularly when dealing with grief issues.

When beginning a group it is very important that each member feel safe. Setting clear expectations helps. The facilitator is obligated to manage the group process, model respectfulness and, if necessary, be available as a resource for support between sessions.

When working with groups, there is a delicate balance between paying attention to the individual who is speaking and the rest of the group. It may be useful to think of the group as the client, remembering that the group is composed of individuals. Setting the tone during informational conversations prior to the start of the group is valuable. The first session creates the environment for the entire group, so attention to details and modeling respectful listening is essential. Appropriate personal sharing by the facilitator usually enhances the sense of safety that group members need to experience.

Grief needs to be handled in an extremely sensitive way, especially in a group setting. It is important not to open an issue that cannot be fully explored and closed in that session. When we work with people who are grieving, we must provide a safe haven for those going through one of the most difficult periods of life. While grief is a natural reaction to a loss, each of us has an innate capacity to heal from grief and loss; the duration and intensity of grief are unique for each individual. Caring and acceptance assist in the healing process.

Being genuinely present with those who are grieving often communicates the most powerful form of support and involves a willingness to tolerate and empathize with the pain. This suggests to the grieving teen that the loss is real and appropriately painful. Being present, listening and caring, communicates confidence that with support, healing will occur.

BRAINSTORMING

Brainstorming is an excellent way to start group members talking and thinking about a particular topic. It is helpful to brainstorm possible solutions to problems or dilemmas. Many of the activities in the book suggest brainstorming with the group.
Before beginning any brainstorming activity, remind the group of the rules for good brainstorming:

- No judging
- Any idea can be added to the list
- No idea is a bad idea
- Hold off discussion of ideas as they are being generated
- Silly or 'off the wall' ideas are good because
    — they may be real solutions for some people
    — they help stimulate creative thinking
    — they break tension

Remind the group that they can be as silly, creative or practical as they wish. Encourage the group members to write down the ideas that appeal to them.

(Continued on the next page)

Facilitation Tips *(Continued)*

JOURNALING

Journaling is a time-honored way to help people sort out their thoughts and feelings. Many different techniques can be used to begin a journaling practice. One way is to set aside some time each day – maybe 15 to 30 minutes in the morning – to simply write whatever comes to mind. Another way is to pick up a journal and write when the person has a 'thinking loop' that seems stuck. In the act of writing, often the thought or situation will lose its intensity. Others find that journaling is a substitute for 'talking.' Some people use their journals as a way of writing letters to their loved ones.

Many people find that they are surprised at how their thinking has evolved when they re-read their journals. For most people the changes that they are experiencing are subtle. Often people grieving do not realize the hard work that they have done, nor do they recognize the changes they have made.

Re-reading a journal can provide an opportunity for self-appreciation.

CLOSING RITUALS

It is useful to establish a ritualized way to end each group session. Group participants will come to expect and appreciate the consistency of how the group process is managed. Ending rituals for each session can be informal, with the facilitator simply making the same statement at the end of each session, or asking the same question of the group. One possibility is to ask participants, about five minutes before the end of the session, to share what, if anything, was particularly helpful during the session.

It is important to create a special ritual or ceremony to end the group during the last session since members have shared intimacies and need to end this part of their relationship, honoring the process. Open the last session in the usual format and proceed as you normally would. Allow sufficient time for your closing ceremony.

One closing ritual is to invite participants to light a tea candle and place it in a bowl of water. After floating the candle in the bowl, each shares a comment on any one of these ideas/topics:

- what has been most beneficial for them, or
- the most important thing they learned during the course of the group, or
- what they learned about the relationship with their loved one, or
- what they learned about themselves

This is done as the very last activity, so any activities, discussion, and filling out evaluations (if you are using evaluations) are completed first.

To the Facilitator
Taking Care of YOURSELF!

Therapists usually focus on their clients' problems, often forgetting to attend to their own needs. Taking care of yourself benefits you, plus your family, friends and clients!

Here are some reminders:

- Understand you are a catalyst for change (not responsible for making change happen)
- Relax away from work
- Do not take work or clients' issues home
- Engage in hobbies and activities, leaving the problems at work
- Know that it's OK to cry about clients' problems
- Avoid compassion fatigue
- Allow yourself to learn and grow from your clients (know that you will!)
- Be aware of your symptoms of exhaustion
- Keep yourself healthy with exercise, good nutrition and meditation
- Focus on clients' strengths
- Have a realistic view of your role and resilience
- Be aware that it is a privilege, though stressful, to journey with those who have had a loss
- Turn off 'therapeutic mode' with family and friends
- Know that you make a difference
- Use humor as appropriate
- Spend time away from work
- Consult with other professionals regularly; it is OK to ask for help and/or advice
- Belong to professional organizations for support and continuous updating in your field
- Be involved in your community
- Take time off for a vacation, in town or out of town
- Diversify friendships beyond people in your field to develop other perspectives and appropriate distance from daily work
- Avoid hidden grief (those mourning who keep the loss or feelings to themselves). This is common among professionals who are concerned that they may lose their credibility if they openly grieve.
- Create balance in your life between . . .
    - Giving and receiving
    - Attention to family and self
    - Involvement and detachment
    - Feelings of power and powerlessness
    - Clients' needs and your own needs
    - Time spent with people and time spent alone
- Recognize that each client grieves differently and at various paces.

"Compassion and love, the most important human characteristics, live within us all. During times of great turmoil, whether it is a horrific tragedy involving massive death or whether it is a single incident of a family experiencing the death of one child, compassion must move from dormant to active. The families of tragedies will still suffer, for you can never take away their pain. But a compassionate community will not add burden and further injury to their immense suffering and will make the healing journey a bit easier to endure. Love your job, love your family, love your country, and love one another."

— *Elisabeth Kübler-Ross*

SECTION II — CHAPTER 1

Let's Get Started

INTRODUCTION FOR THE FACILITATOR

The purpose of this chapter is to lay the foundation for grief education and/or support group. It is of utmost importance that at the first meeting (and during any informational and/or screening contacts) all teens feel welcomed, valued and safe. Creating a space that is safe, accepting and comfortable will enable teens to share freely.

Maintain a stance of acceptance while remaining alert for signs that a group member may need additional therapeutic assistance. Teens should NEVER be coerced into sharing thoughts or feelings. If any of the teens consistently choose not to share, it may be wise to meet with that person alone to discuss the process and ask if he or she is benefiting from listening to others. His or her presence and listening may be a way of participating.

If any of the teens display behaviors or share thoughts that the facilitator finds disturbing, a private conversation with that person is in order. One of the functions that group facilitators provide is the identification of persons who may need individual counseling. Referrals are appropriate and facilitators should have a list of qualified counselors in their area they can make available to participants.

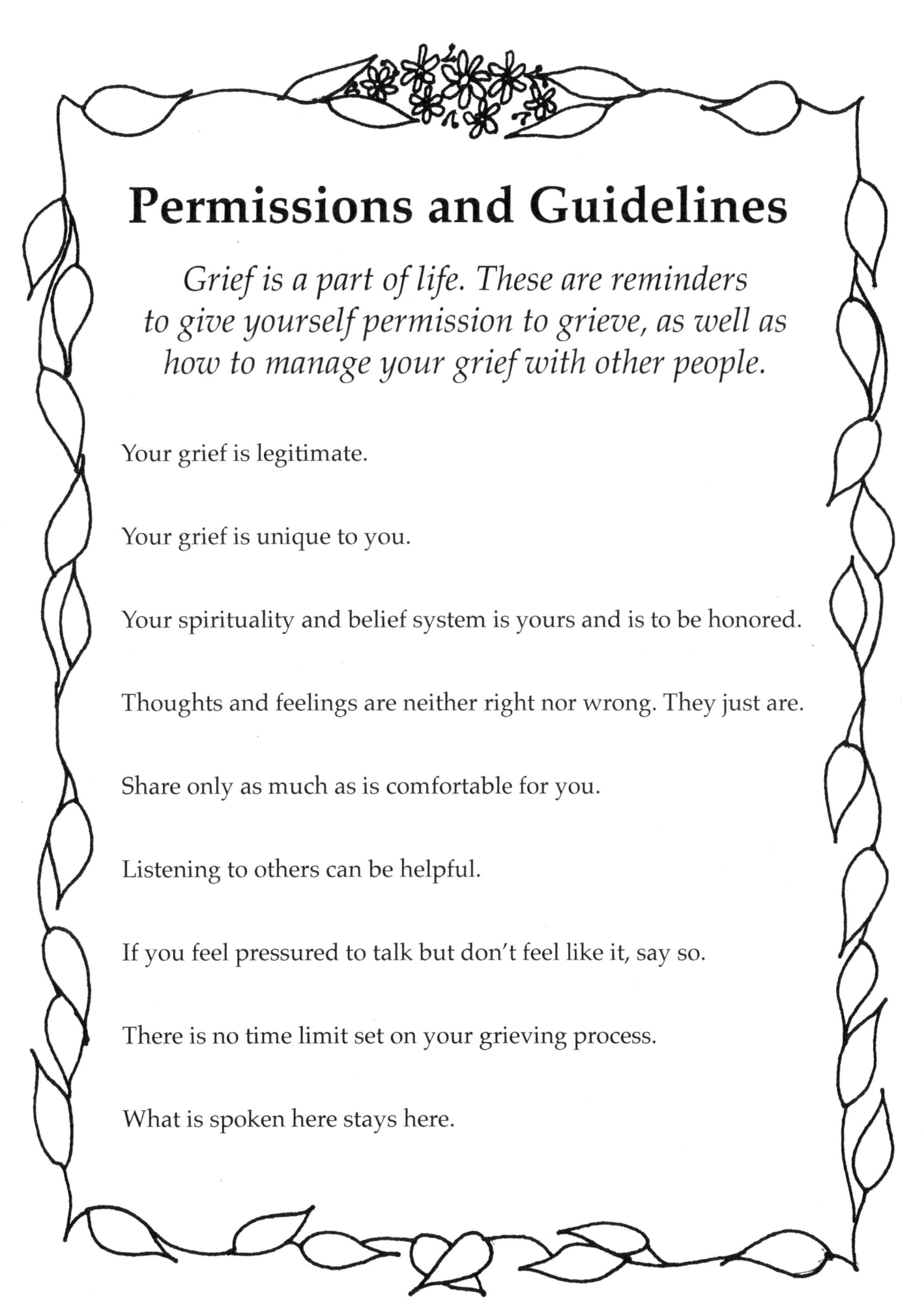

Permissions and Guidelines

Grief is a part of life. These are reminders to give yourself permission to grieve, as well as how to manage your grief with other people.

Your grief is legitimate.

Your grief is unique to you.

Your spirituality and belief system is yours and is to be honored.

Thoughts and feelings are neither right nor wrong. They just are.

Share only as much as is comfortable for you.

Listening to others can be helpful.

If you feel pressured to talk but don't feel like it, say so.

There is no time limit set on your grieving process.

What is spoken here stays here.

PERMISSIONS AND GUIDELINES

PURPOSE

When beginning a group it is very important that each member feel safe. Having clear expectations helps. The facilitator is obligated to manage the group process, model respectfulness and, if necessary, be available as a resource for support between sessions. Confidentiality and respectful behavior should be emphasized.

ACTIVITY

Distribute the handout and ask each teen to read one statement aloud, or give each person an opportunity to read the handout to themselves. After the handout has been read, underscore the importance of these guidelines and ask if anyone can think of other guidelines that the group may want to adopt.

Post the final consensus of group guidelines in the meeting space. Ask group members to sign the guidelines and make a commitment to uphold respect for the group.

Ribbon Activity

Imagine each ribbon in the basket represents a different aspect of the grief process.

You can select the ribbon that is related to how you are feeling today and what is meaningful to you now. You may select more than one ribbon, and you may be thinking about more than one person as you select ribbons.

You can share as much or as little, as you like.

The ribbon colors and their meanings are:

- BLACK — Recent loss, active grieving
- PURPLE — Disorganization, early stage of moving forward
- GREEN — Healing, moving forward
- BLUE — Anniversary of the loss or another memory trigger
- WHITE — Unsure of where I stand

RIBBON ACTIVITY

PURPOSE

This activity is a nice way for group members to introduce themselves. It provides a framework, allowing participants to say as little or as much as they like. It is wise to review group rules and talk about confidentiality prior to this introductory activity (see PERMISSIONS AND GUIDELINES, page 19). The ribbon pieces should be long enough for the participants to tie around their wrists.

ACTIVITY

After reviewing the meaning associated with each ribbon color, invite participants to approach the basket, one at a time, state their name and select the ribbon(s) that they wish. They can then tell the group why they picked those particular ribbons. Remind the group that they can select more than one ribbon and think about more than one person. Another option is that teens can journal the reason why they selected those colors.

THE HEALING PATHWAY

The journey from Loss to *New Normal* is a long, winding and complicated one. There are markers along the way to help you better understand the characteristics of the phases of the grieving process.

SHOCK - THE REALITY OF THE LOSS HAS NOT SUNK IN

Some symptoms of SHOCK:
- Disbelief
- Numbness
- Searching
- Suicidal thoughts*

DISORGANIZATION - THE REALITY OF THE LOSS IS REAL

Some symptoms of DISORGANIZATION:

- Accident prone
- Aimlessness
- Anger
- Anguish
- Anxiety
- Apathy
- Avoidance
- Childlike behavior
- Confusion
- Depression
- Diffulty concentrating
- Fear
- Forgetfulness
- Guilt
- Hopelessness
- Internal conflict
- Isolation
- Loneliness
- Loss of appetite
- Loss of faith
- Loss of interest
- Loss of meaning
- Nightmares
- Physical distress
- Preoccupation
- Relief
- Restlessness
- Risky behavior
- Sadness
- Sleeplessness
- Slowed reaction time
- Suicidal thoughts*

REORGANIZATION - REBUILDING A SATISFYING LIFE – *New Normal*

Some symptoms of REORGANIZATION:
- Ability to remember the good and bad
- Hope for the future
- New priorities
- Pleasure in remembering
- Return to or surpass previous levels of functioning

These symptoms are NOT checklists. These are *some* of the symptoms that *some* people feel *some* of the time. Every person's experience of grief is different and each has different feelings and reactions. Remember, THE HEALING PATHWAY is not a one-way or one-lane path. There is potential for a great deal of movement among the phases as we move towards a *New Normal*, which is constantly changing.

*** If you have suicidal thoughts, seek professional help immediately.
The National Suicide Prevention Life-line telephone number is 1-800-273-8255.**

THE HEALING PATHWAY

PURPOSE

The purpose of THE HEALING PATHWAY is to provide a framework and a common language for talking about the grieving experience without timelines or pathology. This educational handout is a tool to use as the facilitator thoroughly explains the concept of THE HEALING PATHWAY, pages 11–12. Participants need to understand the concept so that grief is not looked upon as pathological. It is important to remind participants that the *New Normal* is their own personal *New Normal* and is constantly changing.

The purpose of THE HEALING PATHWAY is to help teens establish their *New Normal*. By *New Normal*, we are consciously referring to each individual's unique experience. It must be clearly understood that *New Normal* is not a static destination and is unique to each individual. Each teen has a unique way of being in the world. My *New Normal* will be **what is right for me**; your *New Normal* will be **what is right for you**. Developing a *New Normal* – a relatively comfortable way of living in one's current circumstances – is the goal.

ACTIVITY

Distribute this educational handout as you begin to explain THE HEALING PATHWAY. Participants may want to take notes. Refer to this handout throughout the sessions to continue to normalize participants' experiences.

The Healing Pathway

NEW NORMAL

LOSS

"The path to healing from a loss is different for each person, one which may have unexpected twists and turns, but a road that has been traveled by many."

— Kirsti A. Dyer, MD, MS, FT

The Healing Pathway

PURPOSE

This blank Healing Pathway can be used either as a handout or enlarged and used as a poster, laminating it after enlarging. The poster will serve as an excellent prop when discussing The Healing Pathway.

ACTIVITY

As a group activity, everyone can color sections of The Healing Pathway poster. This would be useful as a team-building activity if the group needs to develop some cohesiveness. Individual participants can be creative and color The Healing Pathway handout in ways that are meaningful to them.

Another possibility is to ask participants where on The Healing Pathway the different phases are (shock, disorganization and reorganization) and where they see themselves. This can also be done using the tasks (accepting the loss, feeling the feelings, adjusting and moving forward.)

As a visual, group members can put a sticky note with their name, where they are on the path. Give them the option to move their sticky note as the meetings continue.

Grief Is Like a River

My grief is like a river, I have to let it flow,
but I myself determine just where the banks will go.

Some days the current takes me in waves of guilt and pain,
but there are always quiet pools where I can rest again.

I crash on rocks of anger; my faith seems faint indeed,
but there are other swimmers who know that what I need

Are loving hands to hold me when the waters are too swift,
and someone kind to listen when I just seem to drift.

Grief's river is a process of relinquishing the past.
By swimming in hope's channels, I'll reach the shore at last.

~ Cinthia G. Kelley

TASKS OF HEALING FROM A LOSS

Four tasks are related to the work of grieving.
Personal growth and healing are built on these tasks.

1. **ACCEPTING THE LOSS** is the starting point for the work of grieving. Accepting the loss refers not only to intellectual acceptance, but to emotional recognition. Intellectual acceptance occurs as a person emerges from *shock*. The full emotional acceptance may take longer and occurs as the other tasks are being accomplished.

2. **FEELING THE FEELINGS** is counter-intuitive for many teens. They would rather deny feelings, push them aside, distract themselves and/or 'stuff' them instead of experiencing the full weight of any uncomfortable feelings and concerns. Experiencing emotions, including fear and confronting change, is essential to the healing process. This is a primary task during *disorganization*.

3. **ADJUSTING** relates to learning to live without whatever or whomever is no longer present. Reorganizing one's life depends on the nature of the loss. We associate this process with the stage of *reorganization* along THE HEALING PATHWAY.

4. **MOVING FORWARD** is when we notice that the grieving teen has been able to adjust in a way that allows for personal growth. Moving forward does not imply forgetting. It is recognition of living life fully, being grateful for the loved ones and all that we do have, with a genuine capacity for joy, in a newly constituted way and formulating a vision for the future. This coincides with the concept of *NEW NORMAL*.

TASKS OF HEALING FROM A LOSS

PURPOSE

This educational handout is intended to be used with THE HEALING PATHWAY, page 23. It is a slightly altered version of the facilitator's information on page 13.

ACTIVITY

After discussing THE HEALING PATHWAY, distribute this handout and discuss, relating the tasks to the phases on THE HEALING PATHWAY. Remind the group members that the path has many twists and turns, and is not a one-way street.

I can choose to sit in perpetual sadness,
immobilized by the gravity of my loss, or
I can choose to rise from the pain and treasure
the most precious gift I have – life itself.

~ Walter Anderson

Rights of Teens Experiencing Grief

- *I have the right to experience my own unique grief in my own unique way.*
- *I have the right to feel what I am feeling, regardless of how those feelings shift from moment to moment.*
- *I have the right to feel angry.*
- *I have the right to ask "why."*
- *I have the right to ask for privacy.*
- *I have the right to ask for help.*
- *I have the right to be listened to.*
- *I have the right to be treated with respect.*
- *I have the right to socialize when ready.*
- *I have the right to cry – or not.*
- *I have the right to express my feelings in a helathy way.*
- *I have the right to be upset.*
- *I have the right to be supported.*
- *I have the right to respectfully express my needs.*
- *I have the right to talk about my grief.*
- *I have the right to experience joy.*
- *I have the right to feel a multitude of emotions, or not.*
- *I have the right to be tolerant of my physical and emotional limits.*
- *I have the right to experience unexpected bursts of grief.*
- *I have the right to make use of healing rituals.*
- *I have the right to embrace my spirituality.*
- *I have the right to have fun.*
- *I have the right to be disappointed.*
- *I have the right to search for meaning.*
- *I have the right to treasure my memories.*
- *I have the right to be given time for the healing process.*

RIGHTS OF TEENS EXPERIENCING GRIEF

PURPOSE

This handout is designed to help teens experiencing grief understand their rights and normalize their experience. Since it is a new experience or situation, and because emotions are raw, it is sometimes confusing to know what is okay.

ACTIVITY

It will be helpful to review this handout at the beginning of your sessions and elicit comments from the teens. Ask each participant to read a line. The facilitator can also explain that these are the rights that the authors came up with, and challenge the individual or group members to think of additional rights. They can write those rights on the back of the handout and take it home, posting it in a visible spot, where they can be reminded of their rights.

We deliberately did not number this list so as not to imply ranking. However, when using this handout in a group, it might be helpful for you to have the list numbered, to better refer to each one. If so, number them prior to reproducing the page.

SECTION II — CHAPTER 2

Getting in Touch

INTRODUCTION FOR THE FACILITATOR

Before teens can "move through their feelings," they need to know what they are experiencing. The purpose of this chapter is to help teens develop a language and an ability to recognize what they are feeling. Many people believe that the best way to cope with unpleasant feelings is to ignore or 'stuff' them. This is not true. In spite of the counter-intuitive nature of this, teens need to be encouraged to sit with and feel what they are feeling. The more this is done, the greater the likelihood that they will see that feelings wax-and-wane, and the capacity for pleasant feelings exists along side of difficult ones.

Teen GriefWork Emotions

Check the emotions you are experiencing right now.

"I feel ..."

Cautious ❏	Annoyed ❏	Loved ❏	Lonely ❏	Discouraged ❏	Jealous ❏
Frustrated ❏	Helpless ❏	Hostile ❏	Apathetic ❏	Disappointed ❏	Numb ❏
Relieved ❏	Confused ❏	Restless ❏	Sad ❏	Judged ❏	Hysterical ❏
Hopeless ❏	Guilty ❏	Anxious ❏	Angry ❏	Forgetful ❏	Regretful ❏
Disconnected ❏	Miserable ❏	Unsupported ❏	Yearning ❏	Shocked ❏	Capable ❏
Aimless ❏	Denial ❏	Acceptance ❏	Fear ❏	Hopeful ❏	Determined ❏
Supported ❏	Unfocussed ❏	Overwhelmed ❏	Needy ❏	Resilient ❏	Abandoned ❏

© 2012 WHOLE PERSON ASSOCIATES, 101 WEST 2ND STREET, SUITE 203, DULUTH MN • 800-247-6789

GRIEFWORK EMOTIONS

PURPOSE

Teens are capable of experiencing a wide variety of emotions at any given time. Recognizing this can be empowering. People can begin to appreciate just how difficult the grieving process can be when they take the time to notice the different emotions they feel and the fact that they can experience any number of them at the same time. Grief will subside over time; however, the grieving process does not happen in a step-by-step or orderly fashion.

ACTIVITY

This handout can stimulate teens to identify and name some of their emotions. Encourage participants to notice what they are feeling and check those emotions on the handout. Teens can take the handout home, and at various times during the next few days, repeat the exercise, checking it off with an "X", a "√", or different color markers. They might want to track the time of day these feelings emerge. A particular emotion may be of significance to them in their disrupted life routine, or heighten their awareness of specific times of the day that are best for them, or help them notice particularly vulnerable times of the day. This will emphasize the point that people feel different emotions constantly – many at the same time – many in the same day. When they allow themselves to fully experience what they are feeling, the emotions tend to shift, sometimes slightly and sometimes dramatically.

This handout works very well with EMOTIONS SALAD BOWL, page 35, and is an excellent reference sheet for many of the activities in this book. GRIEFWORK EMOTIONS can be enlarged on a photocopy machine and used as a poster.

The Emotions Salad Bowl

Grieving can be difficult because we feel many emotions at once.

Under some of the salad ingredients write the emotions you are feeling now.

Having many different emotions at the same time adds to the richness of our lives and makes for a much more interesting salad!

THE EMOTIONS SALAD BOWL

PURPOSE

Recognizing the variety of simultaneous emotions can be empowering. Teens begin to appreciate how difficult the grieving process can be when they notice their array of emotions. In the salad bowl metaphor, variety is the 'spice of life'. Participants will become aware and recognize the different emotions they feel, all at the same time. Just as the wide variety of ingredients in a salad — with different textures, colors and tastes enliven a salad and make it more interesting — the different emotions we experience simultaneously, enliven and enrich our lives. This handout works well in conjunction with GRIEFWORK EMOTIONS, page 33.

ACTIVITY

Discuss the salad bowl metaphor. Ask members of the group to write an emotion that they have felt today under each of the vegetables. Then ask the group to share the emotions they wrote on the paper. Note if participants share similar emotions.

Depending on the age of the group members and size of the group, you may choose to use real, tangible items for this metaphor. This creates a visual and tangible activity. Handouts may be used to journal.

Serenity Prayer

Grant me the serenity to

Accept the things I cannot change . . .

_____

_____

_____

_____

Courage to change the things I can . . .

_____

_____

_____

_____

And the wisdom to know the difference.

SERENITY PRAYER

PURPOSE

It is important for teens to realize just what they have control over and what they cannot change. This activity will facilitate thinking about these differences. It can be used in conjunction with CONTROL, page 39.

ACTIVITY

Acknowledge that the SERENITY PRAYER, popularized by the recovery community, has great validity for all of us. It is a good starting point for discussion. It is important to discuss the differences between the categories – knowing what a person has control over, no control over and what he/she can change.

Allow participants time to complete the handout and invite them to share. Encourage a continuation of the activity with a discussion about action steps needed to make the realistic changes.

Control

THINGS I CAN CONTROL
example: my attitude

THINGS I CANNOT CONTROL
example: the loss

Control

PURPOSE

It is important for teens to realize the limits of what they can control. Remind the group that we only have control over our own responses and reactions.

ACTIVITY

You may use this handout in a group setting to stimulate thinking. Prior to giving each person a copy, have a general discussion about what people can and cannot control. Distribute the handouts and allow two to five minutes for participants to write their thoughts. When they finish, have the group discuss what they wrote. Some people may find that their own thinking is stimulated by what others share.

It is beneficial to use this handout in conjunction with SERENITY PRAYER, page 37.

You have no control over what the other guy does.
You only have control over what you do.

~ A. J. Kitt

FEAR

Fear is a normal response to loss – fear of the unknown, fear of the unfamiliar and fear of the changes in your life.

What do you fear? _____
_____

What are you avoiding because of this fear? _____
_____

What else may be adding to this fear? _____
_____

What steps could you take to work through this fear? _____
_____

- -

What do you fear? _____
_____

What are you avoiding because of this fear? _____
_____

What else may be adding to this fear? _____
_____

What steps could you take to work through this fear? _____
_____

- -

What do you fear? _____
_____

What are you avoiding because of this fear? _____
_____

What else may be adding to this fear? _____
_____

What steps could you take to work through this fear? _____
_____

FEAR

PURPOSE

Many teens are reluctant to realize that they are fearful, and even when they can or do admit this to themselves, they are not able to identify what the fears are about. People often recognize that they are angry, anxious or even depressed, but are unaware that fear may be at the root of those feelings. Teens who experience any type of loss may wonder – how does this affect my life and how will I cope?

The first step is to identify what is so frightening. Giving voice to these and other fears is very helpful in dealing with a challenge and acknowledging that there is a challenge. It is after getting in touch with these difficult feelings that people can begin to work through them.

It is a goal for the facilitator to help normalize the fears that are so common when one is grieving.

ACTIVITY

Introduce this activity using the explanation above, and then encourage teens to face their fears by sitting quietly, allowing them the time and emotional space to recognize one of those fears. Some may need to re-phrase this to "something that I'm afraid of" or "something that scares me." Give adequate time and then encourage sharing. If participants are open to it, you may invite others in the group to help with brainstorming ways to manage the fear.

No one ever told me that grief felt so much like fear.

~ C.S. Lewis

My Regrets

We all experience losses in our life, and it is common to have regrets.

Identify your recent loss: _____

Finish the sentence-starters below that apply to you and this loss:

I'm sorry I _____ .

I knew _____ .

We didn't talk about _____ .

I wish _____ .

I never should have _____ .

If only I _____ .

How could I have _____ .

Why didn't _____ .

I wish I had _____ .

I am angry _____ .

I did not honor the request that _____ .

I still get upset about _____ .

When I think back I _____ .

My Regrets

PURPOSE

The purpose of this handout is to help teens recognize that regret and/or feelings of guilt can be debilitating — therefore it needs to be put in perspective. If the regret or guilt felt is realistic and reasonable then the goal would be to learn from it and forgive oneself. Often these feelings are unreasonable, born out of unrealistic expectations. It is important to recognize these feelings, and acknowledge and honor them, learn to let them go.

ACTIVITY

The nature of regret and guilt should be explored prior to distributing the handout. Suggest the use of substitute words, like "sorry," "guilty," or phrases like "I feel bad about…"

When one door closes, another opens; but we often look so long and so regretfully upon the closed door that we do not see the one which has opened for us.

~ Alexander Graham Bell

We must all suffer from one of two pains: the pain of discipline or the pain of regret. The difference is discipline weighs ounces while regret weighs tons.

~ Jim Rohn

If only. Those must be the two saddest words in the world.

~ Mercedes Lackey

You're Not Alone

It is comforting to know that grief symptoms happen to everyone.

Which do you recognize?

❑ I am unable to concentrate

❑ I don't want to go anywhere

❑ I feel angry and/or irritable

❑ Nothing interests me

❑ I am upset that the world goes on as normal

❑ I hear a familiar song and cry

❑ I feel like I am losing my mind

❑ I do not want to get out of bed in the morning

Additional grief symptoms that happen:

❑ _____

❑ _____

❑ _____

❑ _____

❑ _____

❑ _____

❑ _____

❑ _____

Where do you think you are right now on THE HEALING PATHWAY?

❑ Shock

❑ Disorganization

❑ Reorganization

YOU'RE NOT ALONE

PURPOSE

This activity can be used to help teens recognize some of the common symptoms of grief. It can be used to help them assess their progress along THE HEALING PATHWAY by noting their symptoms and how they correlate to the various phases. Be sure to use THE HEALING PATHWAY, page 23, prior to this handout.

ACTIVITY

Introduce this activity with the reminder that everyone experiences grief in different ways and there are many common symptoms. Some symptoms are physical while others are more emotional or spiritual. Whatever each person experiences is real for that person and needs to be accepted and validated. After a discussion, distribute the handout and allow two to three minutes for participants to finish.

Encourage the group to add other signs and symptoms of their grief. Have group members share some of the additional symptoms they came up with. Included below are some suggestions for the facilitator to use as examples if the group has difficulty getting started, or for further ideas:

- I'll never feel better
- I am overwhelmed
- I only want to be alone
- I misplace things constantly
- I am unwilling to try new things
- I forget what I started to say
- I just want to sleep
- I am tempted to do things I know I shouldn't
- I feel like my life is not 'normal'
- I am unable to describe what is happening to me
- I do not want to be involved in anything, with anyone
- I feel alone when surrounded by loved ones
- I need to talk about my grief issue constantly
- I do not want to talk about my grief issue at all
- I don't know what's wrong with me
- I am instantly saddened
- I have a sense of being cheated
- I smell a familiar aroma and get very upset
- My life stopped when my loss happened
- I become distraught when seeing a resemblance
- I feel sad at the change of a season
- I cannot figure out how to move forward
- I cry for no reason at all

It is also helpful to discuss where the various symptoms are likely to appear along THE HEALING PATHWAY.

What to do with my memories?

Memories to keep and to savor

Memories to put aside and return to later

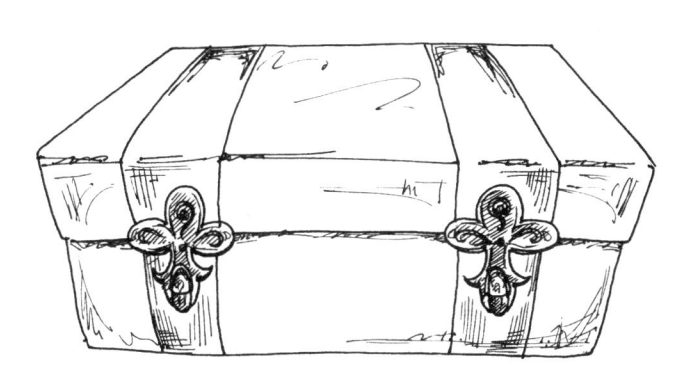

WHAT TO DO WITH MY MEMORIES?

PURPOSE

Memories are very important. It is sometimes confusing because often memories provoke strong feelings – sometimes feelings of sadness because of missing the person and sometimes feelings of relief because of no longer needing to deal with some unpleasant aspect of the person or situation. When something is remembered, smiles or tears may come, depending on what is evoked. The wide range of these emotions is to be expected. Keeping this in mind, it is important to encourage participants to **feel what they feel** and then move on. One way to do this is to treasure memories (even the unpleasant ones), share them with trusted others, or journal about them. They need to notice the feeling and **stay with it**. As they stay with the feeling they will often notice how the feelings shift. The participants may also notice physical sensations, i.e., tightness in the chest, breath changes, etc. Suggest that they make a decision as to what to do with this particular memory – put it in their memory book and savor it, or, perhaps put it aside and come back to it later.

ACTIVITY

After reviewing the above information, distribute the handout. Give the participants five minutes to jot down a few memories which they can put into either category. Have them share one cherished memory with the group. Encourage them to continue filling in the handout at home.

Alternatively, have two boxes in the room marked SAVOR and LATER. Distribute a number of paper strips and ask the teens to write their memories and place them in the appropriate box. At the end of the group meeting, return the SAVOR memories. Hold the LATER memories for another meeting.

SECTION II — CHAPTER 3

Telling Your Story

INTRODUCTION FOR THE FACILITATOR

The value of giving teens who are grieving the opportunity to share their stories cannot be overstated. It is extremely important for teens to process their experiences by talking about them. Journaling is another way of "talking" and at this point, it may be helpful to present teens with a blank journal to use. Teens will benefit by relating details of their story.

Memento Activity

This is a reminder to select any memento to share.

MEMENTO ACTIVITY

PURPOSE

It is very important for teens to have the opportunity to talk about the circumstances of their loss, and focus on accomplishments, attributes or shared activities. This activity is self-directed with the participants deciding on the type of memento or other reminders (pictures from magazines, etc.) they will bring and the information they will share. If they forget to bring a memento, invite them to share a 'virtual' memento, describing the item they forgot to bring.

ACTIVITY

Explain that the homework is to select any mementos that they have and bring them in to share. Ask them to use the mementos as props to tell some things about their loss that they would like others to know.

Using the memento as a prop, the participant can:

- Tell the group about the loss
- Tell the group about the relationship
- Think about and share attributes of the person

WHAT I MISS

WHAT I MISS

PURPOSE

Journaling is an activity that often helps teens sort through memories and feelings. This handout is a journal page-starter.

ACTIVITY

After discussing the general value of journaling, explain the value in reminiscing. It is helpful for grief-stricken teens to remember happier times. Looking back in time provides the opportunity to focus on pleasant memories. This may also provoke a sadness regarding what was lost, however, valuing what was can be quite healing.

Ideas can come from anywhere and at any time.

The problem with making mental notes is that the ink fades very rapidly.

~ Rolf Smith

Part of My Story Is . . .

I am sad when _____

I am angry about _____

I miss _____

I wish _____

At school I _____

I wish I had said _____

I cry when _____

Being alone feels _____

I've discovered _____

It's just too much when _____

I get upset when _____

My friends _____

I hate when _____

I am grateful for _____

I am surprised that _____

I treasure _____

It's helpful when _____

I have learned that _____

It's difficult for me when _____

My family _____

PART OF MY STORY IS . . .

PURPOSE

Journaling is an activity that often helps teens sort through memories and feelings. These sentence-starters will inspire both.

ACTIVITY

After reviewing the value of journaling, encourage participants to use these sentence-starters and expand, if strong memories are flowing, into their journals. Because this activity takes a great deal of time, and rushing through would be counter-productive; distribute this handout after the discussion and complete the first sentence-starter as a group. Encourage participants to complete them at home in their journal or on the reverse of the handout.

When I Experienced the Loss of _____

Most people who are grieving benefit by talking or journaling about what happened as well as their individual relationship with that person or event. Complete these "sentence-starters."

I was _____

_____.

The week before _____

_____.

That day _____

_____.

The day after _____

_____.

The family _____

_____.

At school _____

_____.

My friends _____

_____.

The most difficult part was _____

_____.

I was surprised _____

_____.

I was angry _____

_____.

I hadn't expected _____

_____.

WHEN I EXPERIENCED THE LOSS OF

_____

PURPOSE

Journaling is an activity that often helps people sort through memories and feelings. These sentence-starters will inspire both. It is very important for people to have the opportunity to tell the story of their loss, and their feelings at the time, as often as they need. Many people, well-meaning friends and family members, cannot tolerate hearing the story repeated. Journaling is a wonderful way to continue sorting through memories and feelings. These sentence-starters can help someone who needs a bit of prodding to get started with a journal.

ACTIVITY

After discussing the value of journaling, distribute the handout. Review it and ask participants to complete the first sentence-starter aloud in the group. Allow people who want to participate to expand beyond one sentence if they desire. Encourage them to complete the rest at home.

Journal writing is a voyage to the interior.

~ Christina Baldwin

SECTION II — CHAPTER 4

Self-Care

INTRODUCTION FOR THE FACILITATOR

When teens are grieving, it is quite common for them to over-react or under-react and not attend to thier usual self-care routine. The goal of this chapter is to help teens recognize the need to take care of themselves in all five domains:

- Physical
- Intellectual
- Emotional
- Social
- Spiritual

Self-Care Domains

*In each domain,
list the activities you are doing to take care of yourself.*

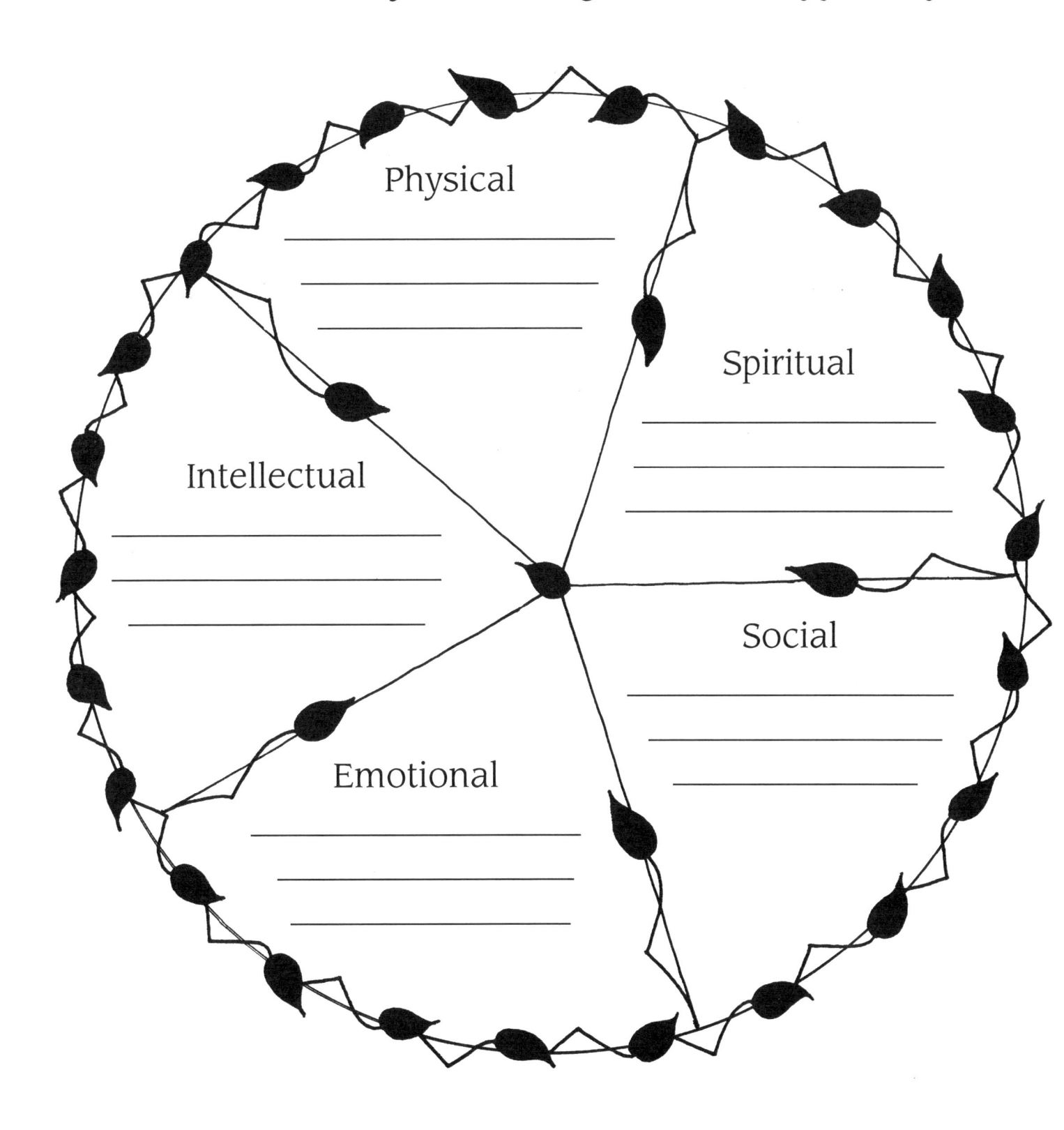

Physical
_____
_____
_____

Spiritual
_____
_____
_____

Intellectual
_____
_____
_____

Social
_____
_____
_____

Emotional
_____
_____
_____

SELF-CARE DOMAINS

PURPOSE

It is important for everyone to understand the need to take care of one's self in all five domains of living. This pie chart illustrates that each domain is of equal importance and needs attention.

ACTIVITY

Educate the teens about the importance of all five domains: physical (body), intellectual (mind), emotional (psychological), social (relationships) and spiritual (different for each person). Explain that most people tend to do a reasonable job of taking care of themselves in a few areas while neglecting others. Ask group members to share one or two self-care activities they currently engage in and discuss in which domain(s) they fall. Point out that the same activity could fall into different domains for different people. Distribute the handout as homework. Participants are asked to record what they do for themselves over the course of a week, noting the self-care activity in the appropriate piece of the pie. It is extremely important to help group members understand that many activities will fall into more than one domain. Encourage them to think about the benefit they derive from the activity and list it in every appropriate domain.

At the next session, ask people to report what they learned from this activity.

Some examples are:

Exercising

- *Physical because it is good for my body and my health*
- *Social because I exercise with friends*
- *Emotional because I release some anger and/or frustration when I exercise*

Walking/hiking

- *Physical because of health benefits*
- *Spiritual because I walk in nature and find that to be my spiritual connection*
- *Emotional because walking is a stress-buster for me*

Reading

- *Intellectual because I'm stimulating my brain by thinking*
- *Emotional because I'm reading escape novels*
- *Spiritual because I'm reading uplifting books*

Are You Taking Care of Yourself?

		Yes, I'm doing it!	No, not yet	This is not for me!
1	Are you eating three healthy meals a day?			
2	Are you refraining from risky behavior?			
3	Do you do something to relax every day?			
4	Do you exercise at least three times a week?			
5	Are you keeping up with your schoolwork?			
6	Do you sleep six to eight hours each night?			
7	Are you kind to yourself?			
8	Do you take your medicines as prescribed?			
9	Are you forgiving yourself?			
10	Do you enjoy poetry and/or spiritual readings?			
11	Are you spending time with supportive friends?			
12	Are you journaling?			
13	Are you balancing between "being" (feeling your feelings) and "doing" (keeping busy)?			
14	Are you asking for help when you feel overwhelmed?			
15	Are you communicating your feelings to others in a healing way?			

© 2012 WHOLE PERSON ASSOCIATES, 101 WEST 2ND STREET, SUITE 203, DULUTH MN • 800-247-6789

ARE YOU TAKING CARE OF YOURSELF?

PURPOSE

This self-assessment tool can be used to help determine what the teens are doing to take care of themselves and what they are willing to try.

ACTIVITY

After a discussion regarding the need and benefits of self-care, distribute the handout and ask teens to look over the list, checking the appropriate columns. The group can then discuss why the various suggestions on the list are important and how they manage the things that they do. It is also worthwhile to discuss some of the items they judged negatively which might be reframed as self-care. (i.e. sleeping more than usual could be escapism or it could be restorative.)

Ask for a show-of-hands for who checked "No, not yet," for a particular item. Ask when they think they will begin that activity or a comparable one. If participants have additional suggestions for self-care, encourage them to share.

Counting My Blessings

At certain times in our lives it is so easy to focus on the negatives and overlook what we have to be grateful for.

List some of your blessings in the stars.

Review this paper every day to remind yourself of how truly blessed you are.

© 2012 WHOLE PERSON ASSOCIATES, 101 WEST 2ND STREET, SUITE 203, DULUTH MN ▪ 800-247-6789

COUNTING MY BLESSINGS

PURPOSE

It is widely acknowledged that focusing on the positive aspects of life is beneficial. This handout is designed to help teens identify and appreciate their blessings and to focus on gratitude.

ACTIVITY

One way to use this is to give teens several copies with the expectation that they will fill in a minimum of three blessings at the end of each day.

This can be used for "big" blessings like

- family
- community
- good health
- safety

or for the "little" blessings one has during the course of the day like

- seeing a beautiful flower
- feeling the warmth of the sun

Suggest that they keep their completed papers and post them in obvious places, where they can be reminded of the blessings in their lives.

Ways to Nourish Myself
Let the healing begin!

Check 'nourishments' that you would be willing to commit to do in the next month.

On the blank lines add some of your own.

❏ get involved in something new

❏ write in a journal

❏ call a friend

❏ take a long warm bath

❏ listen to music

❏ read

❏ work in the garden

❏ resume this activity_____

❏ _____

❏ _____

❏ _____

❏ _____

❏ _____

❏ _____

❏ _____

❏ do a craft or hobby

❏ exercise

❏ meditate

❏ go to a place of worship

❏ go to a movie, even if I cry

❏ go to a museum

❏ care for a pet

❏ volunteer_____

❏ _____

❏ _____

❏ _____

❏ _____

❏ _____

❏ _____

❏ _____

WAYS TO NOURISH MYSELF

PURPOSE

Some teens do not recognize the various ways that they already take care of themselves, or do not consider some of the things they do as self-nourishing. This handout is designed to help people acknowledge the self-nurturing behavior they already engage in and provide some additional ideas to consider.

ACTIVITY

Discuss the importance of self-care and ask participants to share some of the things they already do to take care of themselves. Ask if anyone did some things in the past that they are no longer doing. Discuss the obstacles to returning to previous activities.

After distributing the handout ask each person to check off those things that they already do and, in the blank spaces, add things they do as "nourishments" that are not on the list. With another color pen, check the things that they are willing to try in the next month, again adding items in the blanks. Have the group share after everyone has completed the handout. This can be used effectively with SELF-CARE DOMAINS, page 61.

Spontaneity and Impulsive Behavior

What are some examples of spontaneity?

_____
_____
_____
_____
_____
_____
_____

What are some examples of impulsive/risky behavior?

_____
_____
_____
_____
_____
_____
_____

SPONTANEITY AND IMPULSIVE BEHAVIOR

PURPOSE

It is very common for teens to be impulsive. When grieving, often teens behave more impulsively than usual. Heightening their awareness of the potential downside of risky behavior while acknowledging the value of spontaneity is very important.

ACTIVITY

Engage the group in a discussion about the difference between spontaneity and impulsive/risky behavior. Distribute the handout and give everyone the opportunity to share and discuss consequences of risky behavior and the ability to be spontaneous while having fun, without being dangerous.

Examples:

SPONTANEITY	IMPULSIVE/RISKY BEHAVIOR
• Going out with friends at the last minute	• Using drugs and/or alcohol
• Sitting at a different lunch table	• Unwanted sex

Accomplishments

Often when grieving, we don't accomplish as much each day as we did previously. Keeping track of accomplishments will be helpful.

DAY	ACCOMPLISHMENTS
Monday	
Tuesday	
Wednesday	
Thursday	
Friday	
Saturday	
Sunday	

ACCOMPLISHMENTS

PURPOSE

Teens who are grieving often feel disoriented, disorganized, and unable to function as usual. Sometimes they truly believe that they are not doing anything at all. This activity is designed to help teens realize that they are getting things done, but probably taking more time and energy than they would like. This will help those who are grieving normalize their experience, honor what they are accomplishing, and be motivated to do a little bit more.

ACTIVITY

After discussing how difficult it is to accomplish seemingly mundane tasks, distribute this handout. Ask group members to complete it during the week. Remind them that distractions, decreased energy and confused thinking at this time mean most tasks may take longer than anticipated.

Being the Best You Can Be

Are these possibilities for you? Write your thoughts next to them.

Exercise to regain energy. _____

Walk proud with shoulders back and a bounce in your step. _____
_____

Find ways to laugh. _____

Nod and/or smile when passing someone. _____

Find something beautiful about each day and focus on it. _____
_____

Make a list of things to do and cross off each as it is accomplished. _____
_____

Make a list of long-term goals. Share them with loved ones. _____
_____

Eat healthy. _____

Drink plenty of water and limit caffeine and sugar. _____

Take time for yourself. _____
_____
_____
_____
_____

BEING THE BEST YOU CAN BE

PURPOSE

This handout is designed to remind teens to think about self-care during grief; this is a time when it takes extra energy that they may not have. This often impacts relationships as well as how they feel about themselves.

ACTIVITY

After discussing the importance of self-care and relating it to the five domains (see SELF-CARE DOMAINS, page 61) ask participants to read this handout and make notations about the things that they can do, things they can add to what they are already doing, or why they are *not* doing them. If they think they are doing a particularly good job in some areas have them note what it is that they are doing well.

A Sacred Space

*A sacred space promotes a sense of healing.
It might be helpful to create a sacred place.*

Where can you find a safe and sacred place? _____
_____

What color would be most soothing? _____
_____

What objects would you keep in this space? _____
_____

What aroma would be pleasing? _____
_____

What music would be comforting? _____
_____

What mementos would you bring into this space? _____
_____

What else would make this space scared? _____
_____

Whom would you trust to see this space? _____
_____

A SACRED SPACE

PURPOSE

For some teens creating a special place for quiet, prayer, meditation or reminiscing can be very healing. This handout is designed to help them envision such a spot.

ACTIVITY

Review the idea of a sacred space as a place to be with one's self and one's thoughts. Explain that it need not take up much room, but that it should be a place where one can be alone, quiet and comfortable. Some teens may want mementos in the space and others may want a soothing space without mementos. Validation of these differences is important. Discuss creative ideas where people can construct such a space and how they can create time to spend in it. Distribute the handout and have group members share their responses once they have finished.

My Prayer

MY PRAYER

PURPOSE

Prayer or meditation can provide an opportunity for a teen to communicate with a higher power — God, spirits, the universe, etc. It can be very useful to journal this monologue. Some people may be angry and yell while others may want or ask for guidance. Still others may want to pour out their hearts.

ACTIVITY

This handout is best used as homework. Encourage teens to let loose and share in any way that they need to. At the next session, follow up with discussion about how it felt.

Source of Healing

Spread over me
the shelter of your peace,
that I might reside there,
through this journey
of sadness and pain
that I might some day
find the strength to return
to life and its blessings.

~ David Feldt

Abraham Joshua Heschel says,

In the act of prayer . . . we restore our own mental health.

Need a Good Cry?

*Crying helps to get the sad out of you!
What can you do to bring those tears on?*

Watch a tear-jerking movie.

Look at photographs.

Talk with people who share your loss.

Hold a special memento and focus on it.

_____
_____
_____
_____
_____
_____
_____
_____
_____
_____

NEED A GOOD CRY?

PURPOSE

For some teens it is difficult to cry. We know that crying can be beneficial in terms of releasing hormones and pent up feelings. Participants who feel blocked and want to cry, but have been unable to, may find this useful. If they are unable to cry, that is okay. It is not imperative that they cry now.

ACTIVITY

Review that crying is a good thing, not only emotionally, but also physiologically. Like laughter, crying releases tension and can help our bodies repair. Discuss with the group how they feel after they cry (relieved, embarrassed, tired, relaxed, etc.). Distribute the handout and ask group members to think of additional ways to get the tears flowing. Ask them if they have any suggestions about specific movies, books or music that might help initiate crying.

There is a sacredness in tears. They are not the mark of weakness, but of power. They speak more eloquently than ten thousand tongues. They are messengers of overwhelming grief . . . and unspeakable love.

~ Washington Irving

It Helps to Smile
but it's not always so easy after a loss. However, humor and laughter are essential to well-being!

Check the suggestions below that you would be willing to try in the next month.

❑ Spend time with people with whom you laugh.
❑ Go to the zoo. Visit the monkeys.
❑ Rent humorous movies.
   (*some favorites:*_____)
❑ Sing a fun song or commercial.
   (*some favorites:*_____)
❑ Enjoy humorous shows on television or YouTube.
   (*some favorites:*_____)
❑ Go to the movies, but check first to be sure it's funny.
   (*some favorites:*_____)
❑ Play board games or cards.
   (*some favorites:*_____)
❑ Purchase a humorous one-a-day calendar.
❑ Dance.

Other ways to keep smiling:

❑ _____
❑ _____
❑ _____
❑ _____
❑ _____
❑ _____
❑ _____
❑ _____
❑ _____

IT HELPS TO SMILE

PURPOSE

So many teens believe that it is not appropriate to smile, laugh or enjoy oneself after a loss. It is our intention to help participants recognize that not only is it okay to have a good time, it is beneficial to healing.

ACTIVITY

Review with the participants that smiles, laughter and humor have healing properties. Not only do they make one feel better but they also help others feel more comfortable. Encourage a discussion of what it has been like to laugh and what some obstacles have been for having moments of joy and pleasure. Discuss the fact that we can have several emotions at one time, referring to GRIEFWORK EMOTIONS, page 33 and EMOTIONS SALAD BOWL, page 35. Invite the group members to complete this handout and discuss their responses. As homework each participant can bring in a recommendation of a funny movie or a joke.

Birds sing after a storm; why shouldn't people feel as free to delight in whatever remains to them.
~ Rose Fitzgerald Kennedy

Don't cry because it's over, smile because it happened.
~ Dr. Seuss – Theodor Seuss Geisel

SELF-TALK

Let's work on positive self-talk.

Read the negative self-talk examples in the left column and fill in the corresponding box with positive self-talk.

MY NEGATIVE SELF-TALK	MY POSITIVE SELF-TALK
Ex: I do everything wrong.	*I do some things wrong. That means I do some things right!*
I am so unsure of myself right now.	
I need to be on time and never late.	
I will not ask for help. It shows I'm incompetent.	
I am so tense all the time.	
It shows weakness if I cry.	
I feel so anxious I can hardly breathe.	
I will never ever get over it.	
I cannot handle this.	
This is impossible.	

SELF-TALK

PURPOSE

Self-talk is internal dialogue — the words we use when we talk to ourselves. Our self-talk often reflects and creates our emotional state. It can influence our self-esteem, outlook, energy level, performance, and relationships. It can even affect our health, determining, for example, how we handle stressful events.

Most people have a self-critical voice that talks almost non-stop. This negative self-talk CAN be replaced by positive self-talk. The things we say to ourselves, silently or aloud, have great influence on our mood, energy, self-esteem and attitude. Our messages influence how we interpret the world and greatly influence our emotional state and the power of the words we use.

ACTIVITY

Discuss the notion of self-talk with the group. Ask group members to share some of the phrases they are aware of saying to themselves. Ask if they have examples to share how the self-talk has impacted them.

Distribute the activity sheet and ask group members to come up with phrases they can use to counter the negative self-talk. Some examples are listed below:

As an additional activity, participants can add their personal negative self-talk in the blank lines of the left-hand column, and then reframe.

MY NEGATIVE SELF-TALK	MY POSITIVE SELF-TALK
I do everything wrong.	*I do some things wrong. That means I do some things right!*
I am so unsure of myself right now.	*I need to remember that I do trust myself.*
I need to be on time and never late.	*Being late isn't the end of the world.*
I will not ask for help. It shows I'm incompetent.	*It is a sign of strength to ask for help. It does not mean that I am not competent.*
I am so tense all the time.	*I have reason to be tense and I can help myself by relaxing!*
It shows weakness if I cry.	*It's all right to cry.*
I feel so anxious I can hardly breathe.	*I can breathe deeply and let go of some of the tension.*
I will never ever get over it.	*This is a long and slow journey and I will heal.*
I cannot handle this.	*I will survive, maybe even thrive.*
This is impossible.	*I can do it. I can do it.*

SECTION II — CHAPTER 5

Relationships

INTRODUCTION FOR THE FACILITATOR

Some teens who are grieving experience changes in friendships. There are people in their lives who will be supportive. They somehow know just what to say or do. Others want to be helpful, but simply do not know what to say or do. On the other hand, some friends seem to fall away.

The pages in this chapter offer an opportunity for teens to realistically look at the changes in their relationships.

Emphasize the use of a name code rather than the person's name or initials. (See page 8.)

MY SUPPORT NETWORK

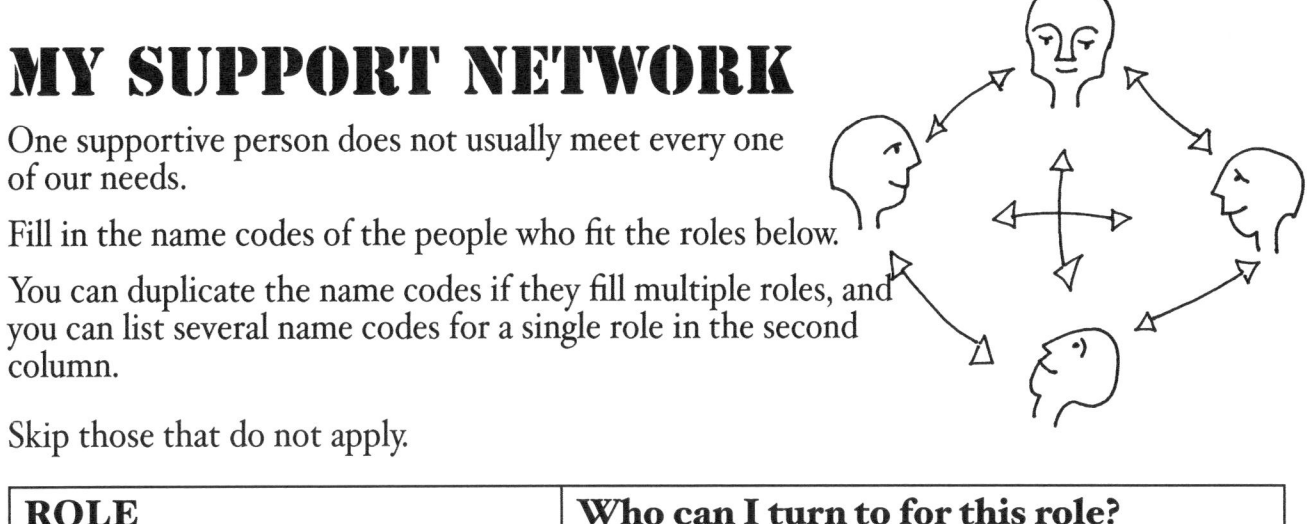

One supportive person does not usually meet every one of our needs.

Fill in the name codes of the people who fit the roles below.

You can duplicate the name codes if they fill multiple roles, and you can list several name codes for a single role in the second column.

Skip those that do not apply.

ROLE	Who can I turn to for this role?
Share problems	
Talk about the loss	
Give good advice	
Energize me	
Have a fun time	
Accept me as I am	
Try something adventuresome, yet safe	
Keep me busy / distracted	
Provide reassurance	
Relax with me	
Meditate with me	
Enjoy a good laugh	
Appreciate the outdoors and nature	
Take a walk	
Go shopping	
Study	
Tell me the truth even if I don't like it	
Work with	
Sit with me at lunch	
Disagree with me when necessary	
Share my spiritual life	
Help with chores	
Do homework	

MY SUPPORT NETWORK

PURPOSE

Often teens who are grieving feel lonely, isolated and confused. It is hoped that this handout will remind group members that they do have supportive people in their lives. This activity can be used in conjunction with SELF-CARE DOMAINS, page 61 and SUPPORT SYSTEM, page 89.

Emphasize the use of a name code rather than the person's name or initials.

ACTIVITY

Brainstorm the types of needs that supportive relationships meet. Remind participants that some needs are met by more than one relationship and seldom does one single relationship help us meet all of our needs. Distribute the handouts and allow participants to complete.

Participants can share answers or discuss which needs are easy to meet and which are more challenging. Problem-solve ways to expand support systems, reminding each of the group members that they have each other too.

The healthy and strong individual is the one who asks for help when he needs it, whether he has an abscess on his knee or in his soul.

~ Rona Barrett

Support System

Seldom does one relationship meet all of our needs.

Name one (or more) person in each category and write the need they fill for you. Skip those that do not pertain to you. (Use name code.)

CATEGORY	NAME CODE	NEED BEING FILLED
Parent		
Grandparent		
Sibling		
Teammate		
Good Friends		
Neighbors		
School Counselor/Therapist		
Clergy		
Club/Group		
Co-worker		
Classmates		
Teacher		
Girlfriend/Boyfriend		
Pet		
Other		

SUPPORT SYSTEM

PURPOSE

Teens who are grieving often feel lonely, isolated and confused. This handout will remind group members that they have supportive people in their lives. This activity can be used in conjunction with MY SUPPORT NETWORK, page 87.

Emphasize the use of a name code rather than the person's name or inititials.

ACTIVITY

Brainstorm with group members the types of needs supportive relationships meet. Refer to SELF-CARE DOMAINS, page 61. Remind them that some needs are met by more than one relationship and seldom does one single relationship meet all of our needs. Distribute the handout and allow participants to complete.

This activity may be overly stimulating for some group members, depending on their loss.

RELATIONSHIPS CHANGE
How have your relationships changed since the loss?

Write the name code of a family member, friend, teacher, counselor or acquaintance in each circle. Put a **+** if it is a positive change, a **−** if it's a negative change, or an **S** for the same.

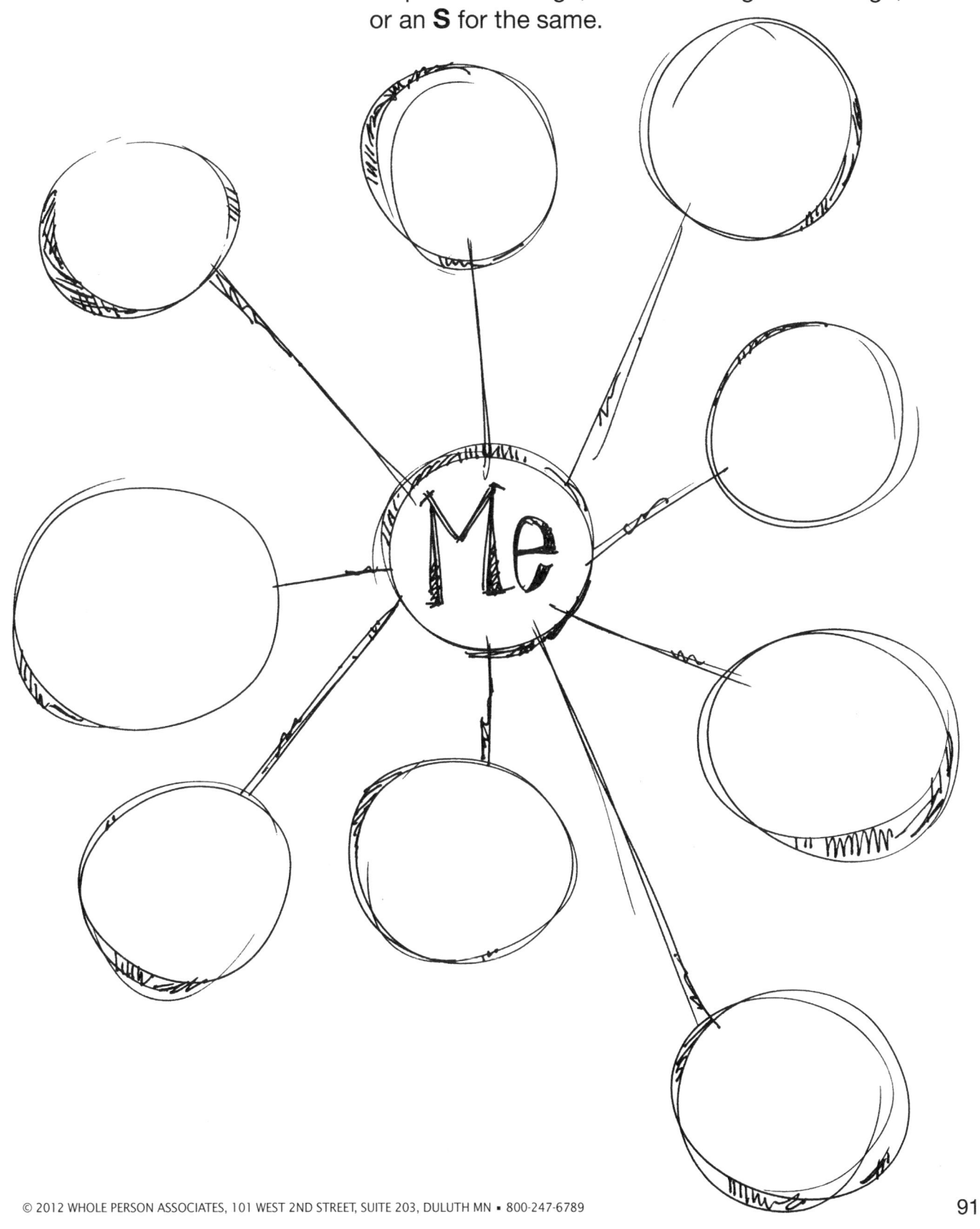

RELATIONSHIPS CHANGE

PURPOSE

Throughout life, relationships change — nothing is static. After a loss, our sensitivities to these changes may be heightened. This activity is designed to help group members be aware of some of the relationships in their lives, and try to see if those relationships have changed, and if so, in what way. The foundation of this exercise is to help the participants notice and accept the movement or shifts that are a part of all relationships.

This is a possible follow-up activity to NOTES TO FAMILY & FRIENDS AFTER A LOSS, page 99.

Emphasize the use of a name code rather than the person's name or inititials.

ACTIVITY

Discuss the nature of relationships in general. Ask participants to think of relationships that they had as young children — maybe a best friend or a beloved teacher. How did that relationship change and shift?

Distribute the handout and ask participants to fill in the name codes of people in their lives. Once that is done, ask them to indicate if the relationship has changed, or stayed the same. Remind the participants that we are comparing the relationship just prior to the loss to the present time.

Some additional questions to pose:

- Are you able to talk to some of these people about your feelings?
- Are you able to reduce the amount of time you spend with those who affect you negatively?
- Do you understand that throughout life relationships change? This may be a time when the changes are more noticeable.
- Do you realize that feeling over-sensitive is common when grieving?

After the handouts are completed, ask group members if they notice a pattern in their relationships and if there is something that they want to do about the pattern. Are there other strategies that they might employ to deal with uncomfortable changes?

Supportive Friends

What do you need in a friend right now?

List a good friend. (Use name code.) _____

Check off if this is true of this friendship:

- ❑ Open communication
- ❑ Acceptance of each other
- ❑ Fun to be with
- ❑ Do not fix or control the other
- ❑ Listen to each other
- ❑ _____

- ❑ Clear boundaries
- ❑ Trust each other
- ❑ OK to have other friendships
- ❑ Give and receive
- ❑ Open to feedback
- ❑ _____

Comments _____

List a good friend. (Use name code.) _____

Check off if this is true of this friendship:

- ❑ Open communication
- ❑ Acceptance of each other
- ❑ Fun to be with
- ❑ Do not fix or control the other
- ❑ Listen to each other
- ❑ _____

- ❑ Clear boundaries
- ❑ Trust each other
- ❑ OK to have other friendships
- ❑ Give and receive
- ❑ Open to feedback
- ❑ _____

Comments _____

List a good friend. (Use name code.) _____

Check off if this is true of this friendship:

- ❑ Open communication
- ❑ Acceptance of each other
- ❑ Fun to be with
- ❑ Do not fix or control the other
- ❑ Listen to each other
- ❑ _____

- ❑ Clear boundaries
- ❑ Trust each other
- ❑ OK to have other friendships
- ❑ Give and receive
- ❑ Open to feedback
- ❑ _____

Comments _____

SUPPORTIVE FRIENDS

PURPOSE

Throughout life, our needs are in constant motion. It may be that this is a time when grieving teens need more support and encouragement than they had needed in the past. Maybe they are the teens who were always giving and do not know how to sit back and receive. Now may be a perfect time to take time for them to look at their friendships and see how they are meeting their needs.

Emphasize the use of a name code rather than the person's name or inititials.

ACTIVITY

Discuss how friendships shift with changing life circumstances. Distribute the handout and instruct participants to use name codes only and fill out the sheet. The facilitator will collect the handouts and cut them apart, mix them up and put them in a basket. Have group members pick a sheet from the basket and read it aloud. Group members can comment. The people who wrote the sheets do not need to reveal their identities.

They Mean Well

People mean well and want to help, but the things they say are sometimes not helpful.

Check any of these that were said to you:

- ❏ How are you doing?
- ❏ It's probably for the best.
- ❏ Don't take it so hard.
- ❏ Why didn't you call me?
- ❏ I know how you feel.
- ❏ It's time to move on.
- ❏ Don't cry.
- ❏ Stay strong for your family.
- ❏ You're so strong.
- ❏ Aren't you over it by now?
- ❏ It will be all right.

What other things have been said to you?

- ❏ _____
- ❏ _____
- ❏ _____
- ❏ _____
- ❏ _____
- ❏ _____
- ❏ _____
- ❏ _____
- ❏ _____
- ❏ _____
- ❏ _____
- ❏ _____
- ❏ _____
- ❏ _____
- ❏ _____

Select several from the list above that are similar to what has been said to you and write how you could respond if it is said to you in the future.

- ❏ How are you doing?   (EXAMPLE) *I'm having a difficult day. Thanks for asking.*
- ❏ _____
- ❏ _____
- ❏ _____

THEY MEAN WELL

PURPOSE

Often well-meaning people say things that upset us. They mean well, but either do not know what to say and are clumsy, or say things they believe will bring comfort, but what ever they do say is not comforting. People sometimes think they are complimenting us, but it may feel like pressure ("You're being so strong"). Sometimes we are stunned by the comment and don't know how to respond. This handout is designed to help grieving teens understand that they will continue to hear those sorts of things; some may be upsetting and others may not. It provides an opportunity to plan and rehearse how to respond.

ACTIVITY

Have a discussion about some of the things that well-meaning people have said that were upsetting. Most groups will have ample examples! Engage the group members in a conversation about what they imagine are the motives behind what is being said. Always emphasize that this mind-reading is our way of making some meaning out of the encounter and that we don't know anyone else's motivation unless we ask. Emphasize the possible positive motives — like he didn't know what to say or she thought she was being comforting. Encourage participants to think about responses that speak to underlying good intentions. During the discussion acknowledge that sometimes saying nothing is perfectly fine.

Distribute the handout and continue the discussion after participants have completed it.

Why Do Friends Drop Away?
Put a check mark by any of the statements that might apply.

- ❑ They may be frustrated because they cannot help me feel better.
- ❑ They have never had a loss like mine and cannot understand my grief.
- ❑ They want me to be done grieving. I'm not.
- ❑ They are uncomfortable with their own feelings, let alone mine.
- ❑ I am not as cheerful as they would like, and they do not want to be pulled down.
- ❑ They are tired of hearing my story, but I still need to tell it.
- ❑ They texted me but I didn't text back.
- ❑ I wanted so much to tell my story. I might have forgotten to listen to them.
- ❑ In every conversation, I think I interject something about my loss. That might get tiresome.
- ❑ I am needier than I used to be.
- ❑ It's hard to stay connected to friends who are far away.
- ❑ _____
- ❑ _____
- ❑ _____
- ❑ _____

WHY DO FRIENDS DROP AWAY?

PURPOSE

Many teens experience the secondary loss of friends who no longer reach out to them. It is helpful for them to understand that this phenomenon is not unique to them.

ACTIVITY

Discuss the commonality of friends dropping away and ask group members to think about experiences that they have had with other losses.

- Were they ever friends with someone who suffered a loss?
- Were they attentive to that friend in ways they now think would be appropriate?
- Have they observed changes in friendships of others who have experienced a loss?

After distributing the handout, ask the group members to each read a sentence. As the sentences are being read, participants should think about their circumstances and check the sentences that they think may apply. Next, ask the group if they can think of other possible explanations for friendships changing.

Brainstorm with the group to think of some ways to maintain contact:

- Call people they haven't heard from
- Make plans and invite someone to join the activity
- Be sure to return calls
- Send an email
- Reach out through social media

Notes to Family and Friends After a Loss

There might be things you would like to say to your family and friends and haven't been able to. Writing your thoughts might help you figure out what you want to say. Then mail, email, call, text, tell them in person, keep in a 'remember' file to look back on, or discard.
(Use name code.)

To	To
To	**To**
To	**To**

NOTES TO FAMILY AND FRIENDS AFTER A LOSS

PURPOSE

This journaling activity is specifically designed to help teens who are grieving articulate anything that they think they should or simply want to say to family and/or friends. The mental fog associated with early grief and the heightened sensitivity that many people experience are likely to cause people to stuff their feelings or spew them inappropriately. This activity helps teens rehearse what they are going to say and how they can say it in a respectful manner. They may feel relief once they have written their message so they no longer feel the need to say it, or the process may clarify just what needs to be said and how it can be done without burning bridges.

Emphasize the use of a name code rather than the person's name or inititials.

ACTIVITY

Discuss the need to communicate feelings, wishes, desires, hopes, dreams and disappointments with family and friends. This needs to be done with some selectivity and mature self-censorship. Ask if there is anyone in their life now to whom they want to say something and have been unable. Explore the reasons for holding back. Acknowledge that reasons for being cautious are important. Let the group know that sometimes it is better to let things go unsaid. The facilitator can then distribute the handout to participants for them to use as a way to . . .

- Sort through personal feelings to determine if they really need or want to say something to a particular person
- Rehearse what to say and how to say it
- Practice asking for help
- Learn to show appreciation
- Get something off their chest

Examples:

To MSS	*To SLN*
You told me you would be there for me. But you only called me once a week and when I tried to talk to you and tell you how I feel about my loss, you just changed the subject and quickly hung up. You didn't spend time alone with me and didn't answer my phone calls. I really needed you and you let me down. I wonder if you know how disappointed I've been.	*You were there for me constantly, for whatever I needed. I hope I have thanked you. I so appreciate everything you have done for me and my family.*

SECTION II — CHAPTER 6

A New Normal

INTRODUCTION FOR THE FACILITATOR

Reorganizing one's life after a major loss is the hope and expectation we have for all teens who are grieving. This *New Normal*, like life itself, is filled with ups and downs; highs and lows; joys and sorrows. The focus of this chapter is to guide the teen who is grieving toward the development of his or her *New Normal*, with a full range of emotions.

The Healing Pathway is the journey; the *New Normal* is the destination. *New Normal* is not a place on the map and is not static — it is constantly evolving. The personal growth experienced while journeying is a predictor of how dynamic the *New Normal* is — and will become.

It is our hope that each teen who is touched by this book will develop a sense of himself or herself as learning, growing and loving in their *New Normal*.

Healing

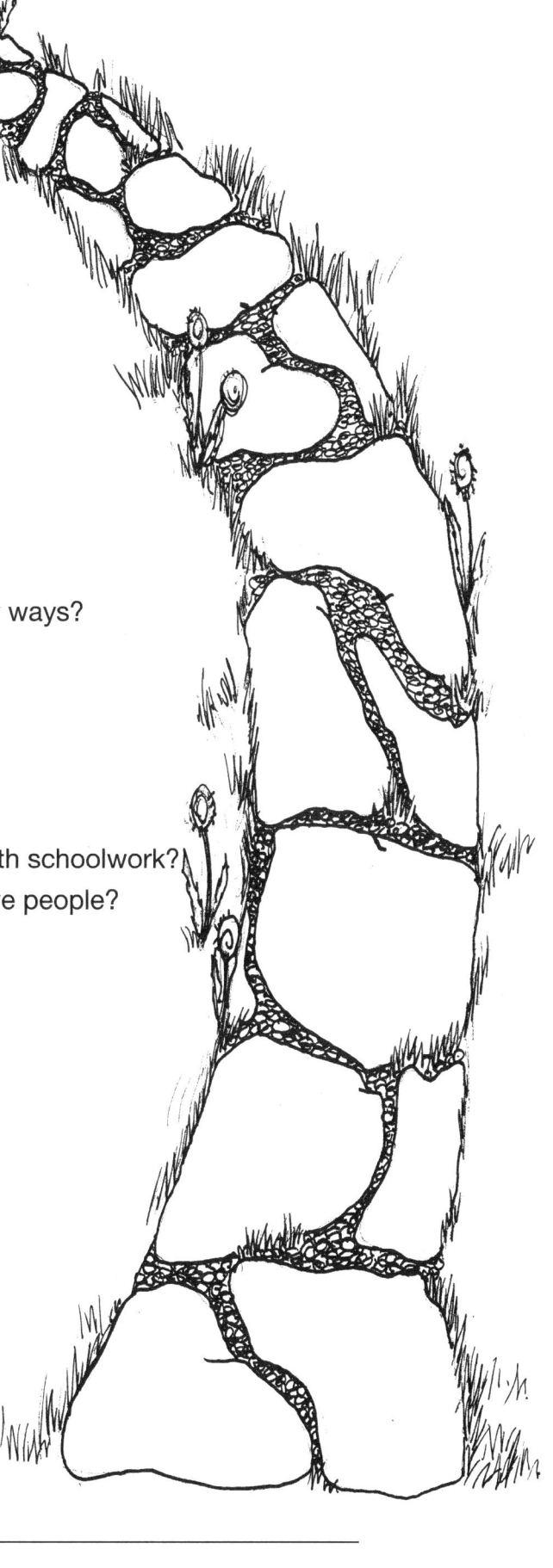

Walking on THE HEALING PATHWAY is an individual process because no two people grieve in the same way. Where are you on the THE HEALING PATHWAY?

Rate these 1, 2, 3, 4 or 5 to see where you are in the process. (1 is no way and 5 is absolutely)

Are you
- ____ forgiving yourself?
- ____ forgiving your loved one?
- ____ moving on with your life?
- ____ releasing uncomfortable emotions in healthy ways?
- ____ finding and accepting support?
- ____ taking care of yourself?
- ____ challenging yourself to learn new skills?
- ____ exercising?
- ____ spending time outdoors in nature?
- ____ getting to school on time and keeping up with schoolwork?
- ____ surrounding yourself with supportive, positive people?
- ____ avoiding addictive behaviors?
- ____ contributing to society?
- ____ doing things that you enjoy?
- ____ giving and receiving hugs?
- ____ actively managing your stress?
- ____ listening to your inner-voice?
- ____ avoiding overly risky behavior?
- ____ taking time to be alone?
- ____ keeping a balanced schedule?

____ TOTAL

The lowest possible total is 20.
The highest possible total is 100.

How do you think you are doing? _____

HEALING

PURPOSE

This self-evaluation is a way to notice progress and become aware of areas that may still need work as the teens continue on THE HEALING PATHWAY towards a *New Normal*.

ACTIVITY

Review the THE HEALING PATHWAY, page 23 and notion of a *New Normal*. Ask participants to consider where they are on their unique HEALING PATHWAY.

Distribute the handout and invite teens to rate themselves in each category. This is a self-assessment and does not need to be shared. It can be used as a group activity or homework. Suggest to participants that they date it and return to it at regular intervals for an updated assessment.

Encourage participants to notice if they are neglecting one of the five life domains. Refer to SELF-CARE DOMAINS, page 61.

Things may not be as good as they were, but they can still be pretty darn good.
~ Harry Rebell

You can cope, or you can cope well.
~ Mae Zelikow

What Has Changed in My Life?

	What Has Changed in My Life?	IT'S A GOOD THING!	IT'S NOT SUCH A GOOD THING!
1			
2			
3			
4			
5			
6			
7			
8			
9			
10			
11			
12			

WHAT HAS CHANGED IN MY LIFE?

PURPOSE

It is often helpful to notice what has changed. Recognizing that life has changed and accepting the changes as part of the new normal, is a significant part of healing and accomplishing the task of moving forward.

ACTIVITY

Discuss life changes with the group. Ask participants to share at least one significant change in their lives and how that change has impacted them. The group will usually come up with the sad, challenging and unpleasant changes. Encourage examples that may be perceived by some as positive to add balance.

Distribute the handouts and allow time for it to be completed. When the group is finished, ask them to share if they have an overall sense of positive or negative changes, or no changes at all. Encourage the participants to revisit this at regular intervals.

For everything there is a season,
And a time for every matter under heaven:
A time to be born, and a time to die;
A time to plant, and a time to pluck up what is planted;
A time to kill, and a time to heal;
A time to break down, and a time to build up;
A time to weep, and a time to laugh;
A time to mourn, and a time to dance;
A time to throw away stones, and a time to gather stones together;
A time to embrace, and a time to refrain from embracing;
A time to seek, and a time to lose;
A time to keep, and a time to throw away;
A time to tear, and a time to sew;
A time to keep silence, and a time to speak;
A time to love, and a time to hate:
A time for war, and a time for peace.
　　　　　　　　　　　　　　~ Ecclesiastes 3:1-8

Coping with Special Days and Holidays

Holidays and special events can be challenging and stressful times during the best of circumstances. They stir up memories of the past, evoke powerful feelings, and force us to compare our life situation to the past and/or to an idealized version.

Dealing with a holiday or special event after a death or loss can become even more difficult. Customary routines are ended, never to be repeated in quite the same way. Holidays can be significant, meaningful and enjoyable — and will be different.

HERE ARE SOME TIPS:

- Try to tell those around you what you need, since they may not know how to help you. Ask for their understanding if you withdraw from an activity that doesn't feel like a good idea to you.

- Acknowledge to yourself that the occasion may be painful.

- Let yourself feel whatever you feel.

- Express feelings in a way that is not hurtful.

- Be aware – grief is emotionally and physically exhausting.

- Take time for yourself for remembrance.

- Honor the memory of a loved one – give a gift or donation in his or her name, light a candle, display pictures and/or share favorite stories with supportive people.

- Discuss, ahead of time with family and/or friends, what each person can do to make this time special.

- Think about what part of this event you are not looking forward to, and discuss with others ahead of time, what can be done to change it.

- Remember, it is okay to laugh and enjoy yourself.

COPING WITH SPECIAL DAYS AND HOLIDAYS

PURPOSE

Holidays and special events like graduations, birthdays, anniversaries, etc. are very difficult to manage for teens who are grieving. They simply may not anticipate the difficulty they may have or the emotions that may be stirred up.

This educational handout should be distributed and discussed whenever a major holiday is approaching, even if it means disrupting the set curriculum for the group.

ACTIVITY

Engage in a discussion of how the teens envision holidays and special events will be. Encourage them to share specific upcoming or anticipated special events in their lives. Ask if anyone has gone through the experience of a celebration since their loss. If a group member is willing, have that person share what it was like and what helped in managing the situation.

Distribute the handout and ask each participant to read a bullet point aloud. Discuss which suggestions seem worth trying.

Bring up the upcoming special day, if there is one, and ask participants if they have thought about how they may honor the day. Encourage group members to begin a conversation with their family, or others with whom they traditionally celebrate, about altering the usual way of doing things.

Holidays and Special Events

Choose five of the sentence-starters below that pertain to you and write in the first thoughts that come to your mind.

My birthday _____.

_____.

On _____, my concern is _____.
    holiday

_____.

Buying gifts is _____.

_____.

Special events (graduations, birthdays, etc.) are _____.

_____.

_____'s birthday is coming up soon and _____.
    name

_____.

On holidays I expect _____.

_____.

Special events feel _____.

_____.

The anniversary of his/her death will be coming soon and _____.

_____.

On holidays I feel obligated to _____.

_____.

The weekends _____.

_____.

© 2012 WHOLE PERSON ASSOCIATES, 101 WEST 2ND STREET, SUITE 203, DULUTH MN • 800-247-6789

HOLIDAYS AND SPECIAL EVENTS

PURPOSE

Helping teens anticipate their reactions gives them an opportunity to plan ways they might not have considered. This handout is designed to help them tap into their feelings and anticipate bumps in the road.

ACTIVITY

Have a discussion of the general upset that may occur with holidays and special events after using COPING WITH SPECIAL DAYS AND HOLIDAYS, page 107. Remind participants of the value of sitting quietly, getting in touch with their feelings, and journaling. Distribute the handout.

Give the members ample time and opportunity to process afterwards, or it may be follow-up homework after a full discussion.

EXAMPLE:

My birthday *will not be as much fun as it was last year*.

Empty House

Going to, or staying at home, can be difficult when a loved one is no longer there.

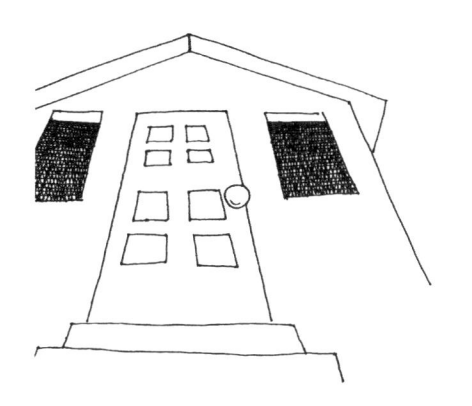

When I am home, I _____

_____

_____

_____

When I am away from the house and going back home, I _____

_____

_____

_____

Other ideas:

_____

_____

_____

_____

_____

_____

_____

_____

EMPTY HOUSE

PURPOSE

This handout is designed to focus on the teen who has had a loss at home, i.e. a death, breakup, divorce, sibling off to college, etc. This loss may also be a beloved pet. Coming home to a house that feels empty is a difficult part of the adjustment to the loss.

ACTIVITY

This is a wonderful handout to stimulate brainstorming. With all brainstorming activities, it is important to remember that the first step is to create a list of ideas, without judging. Once the group runs out of ideas, discuss them with an eye to practicality and desirability. It is imperative to remind all the participants to be respectful. What may be an off-the-wall idea for one person may be the perfect solution for another.

Some possible suggestions might be:

- Bring a friend home from school so the house doesn't feel so empty.
- Play music.
- Curl up where the dog's bed used to be for a short time.

How can I honor _____?

It is said that honoring a deceased person elevates that person's soul. It also helps us feel connected, especially if the manner in which we are honoring the person was important to him/her during his/her life. These also become healing rituals for the survivors.

Here are some ways of honoring a loved one:

- Say a prayer on the anniversary of death.
- Plant a tree.
- Sort through photos and put them in an album with comments written next to the pictures.
- Volunteer time at a place in which the deceased had an interest.
- Create and/or attend a memorial service.
- Celebrate your loved one's birthday in some way.
- Create a sacred space.
- Journal.
- Burn a CD of his/her favorite music.
- Share stories.

Others:

- _____
- _____
- _____
- _____
- _____
- _____
- _____
- _____
- _____
- _____
- _____

HOW CAN I HONOR _____?

PURPOSE

Healing rituals are very important ways that survivors can, in a concrete way, remember their loved one and continue the process of moving on. This handout offers suggestions and encourages thinking about developing personalized rituals.

ACTIVITY

Discuss the benefits of the ritual of remembrance. Ask teens to share any rituals they have performed. Help group members understand that rituals do not have to be religious or culturally specific; any remembrance activity can be considered a healing ritual.

Distribute the handout and encourage teens to share other ideas as they occur to them. Suggest that group members write down those ideas that have some appeal.

I loved just the way

_____
(name)

was, however . . .

I wish _____ .

Why didn't _____ .

If only _____ .

I hated it when _____ .

I am angry about _____ .

I wish _____ could have handled _____ .

I wonder why_____ didn't care about_____ .

Why wouldn't _____ .

and . . . _____

_____

_____

_____

_____

I LOVED JUST THE WAY _____ WAS, HOWEVER…
(name)

PURPOSE

Often when a person is no longer present, the reaction is to idealize that person. Beginning to remember his/her flaws is usually difficult. Sometimes feelings of disloyalty emerge. This handout is designed to help teens who are grieving recognize that these memories add to the full picture of that person and are perfectly normal. Actually beginning to see him/her as a complete person, warts and all, is an indication of movement along THE HEALING PATHWAY.

ACTIVITY

Engage the group in a discussion of how common it is to idealize loved ones and how each person has flaws, eccentricities and habits that may be annoying to family and friends. As the discussion unfolds, see if participants can recognize how they may be idealizing their loved one. You may want to ask the group members to think about the purpose this may serve for them. Discuss the need for a full and balanced picture. Are they able to see some flaws? How do they feel when these thoughts come up?

Distribute the handout and ask participants to select five sentence-starters and complete them. Encourage sharing after the exercise is completed. Remind the group that idealization is very common, serves a purpose, and that seeing the whole picture is not disloyal, it is real.

Example:

> I wish *she would have communicated better with me.*
>
> I wish *he could have been nicer to me.*
>
> I wish *she had a better understanding of my feelings.*
>
> I wish *I had said how I was feeling.*

LOOKING TOWARDS THE FUTURE

One year from today, where do I want to be?

School/Education _____

Extra-curricular _____

Hobby/Activities _____

Work _____

Social _____

Relationships _____

Family _____

Healing _____

Spiritually _____

_____

_____

_____

_____

There is a promise of a brighter tomorrow!

LOOKING TOWARDS THE FUTURE

PURPOSE

It is a sign of health and growth to be looking forward to, and beginning to imagine, what the future will be like without the physical presence of the person the teen misses.

ACTIVITY

Remind the participants of the concept of *New Normal* and The Healing Pathway. Ask them to think about where they currently see themselves on this healing journey. Ask them to describe signs and symptoms of approaching their *New Normal*. Remind them that this is a long and winding path. This handout can be adapted for participants to imagine their future in shorter or longer time-frames. Stress to the participants that they need not take the time-frame literally.

Distribute the handouts and give participants time to do some imagining about their future and write their responses. Invite members of the group to share some of their thoughts after all have completed the handout.

I Have Choices

Decision-making is affected by our emotional state. This is especially true during a stressful period, when it is particularly easy to make impulsive decisions. Every day you have the opportunity to make many choices. Below are some questions to answer as you make decisions. Remember to check in with yourself – pay attention to your responses.

- Am I looking for what is right or am I looking for what is wrong?
- Will this choice propel me toward an inspiring future or will it keep me stuck in the past?
- Will this choice bring me long-term fulfillment or short-term gratification?
- Will this choice increase or decrease my personal energy?
- Does this choice empower me or does it disempower me?
- Is this decision an act of self-love or is it an act of self-sabotage?
- Does this choice promote my personal growth?
- Is this an act of love or is it an act of fear?
- Is this choice in keeping with my values?

A decision I need to make:

_____

My choices:

_____

_____

_____

I Have Choices

PURPOSE

This handout is designed to prompt teens to spend time thinking about the choices they have, the decisions they are making — and will continue to make — as they move forward. It is our intention to guide teens to stop, think, and check in with themselves prior to making decisions. People make most of their decisions out of habitual thinking and reacting. Use this opportunity to help heighten awareness of these patterns and interrupt them.

ACTIVITY

Engage the group members in a discussion about the role that brainstorming choices makes. Ask participants to identify one decision they are facing. Have them list the wide variety of options (choices they have). Encourage them to use the questions on the handout to help them sort through all of the choices to make a decision.

Remind the group that they are presently in a different circumstance and need to check in with themselves about how they feel now, as opposed to how they used to think about the particular situation.

Distribute the handout and encourage teens to keep it available to refer to as situations arise.

You are free to choose, but the choices you make today will determine what you will have, be, and do in the tomorrow of your life.

~ Zig Zigler

Moving Forward

Some goals are so overwhelming!
Breaking them down into steps may be helpful.

What is a goal that you want to accomplish and you just can't seem to get started?
_____

Is it necessary to focus on this goal immediately? _____

When would you like to get it done? _____

When would you want to start? _____

What is the first step in getting this done? _____
_____

How long would that first step take? _____

When will you take the first step? _____

After the first step, when would you be willing to work on it again? _____

What would be the next step? _____

And the next? _____

And the next? _____

Would you like some support or would you prefer to do it alone? _____

If you would like help, who are a few people you would consider asking? _____
_____

How could you reward yourself each time you work on this project? _____
_____

Are you willing to do it? _____ When? _____

MOVING FORWARD

PURPOSE

Breaking goals into steps is often helpful. Analyzing the barriers to completing the goal is also a useful way to move forward and get things done. This handout is intended to help teens clarify actions to accomplish goals.

ACTIVITY

Ask participants to think of one thing that they have wanted to do but have not yet been able to do. Distribute the handout and have them write their goal in response to the first question. They can then answer all of the questions on the page with that goal in mind.

Invite the group members to share what doing this exercise was like for them and any insights they may have gained.

Affirmations

Affirmations are healing, positive statements you say to yourself.

I am moving to a new normal.	*I have the ability to handle this.*
I am taking care of myself.	*I ask for help when I need it.*
I am a special person, unlike anyone else.	*I feel happy at times.*
I am hopeful.	*I am surviving.*
I gain emotional strength each day.	

AFFIRMATIONS

PURPOSE

Affirmations are healing, positive statements that one says to oneself. They are also a way to counter negative self-talk. (Refer to SELF-TALK, page 83.)

ACTIVITY

Discuss the concept of affirmations and the power of saying positive statements to ourselves. Ask participants if they use affirmations, and if so, are they willing to share them. Explain that affirmations are most powerful when we can say them aloud to ourselves in a positive, confident way. Usually they are statements that, on some level, we *know* are true, but we often do not pay attention and sometimes do not believe. This is a way to shift our focus. Ask participants to think of affirmations that they could use.

Distribute the handout and discuss the value of these affirmations. Go around the room asking each person to choose an affirmation printed on the page or one they have written in the blank box, and read it aloud with conviction! Tell the participants to cut them apart and place the affirmations on their bathroom mirror or dresser, dashboard of the car, desk, closet, bedroom or refrigerator door, wallet, books used at home or school, or by the computer. Suggest that they look at them and repeat them throughout the day,

SECTION III

Resources

On the next page is an annotated list of books and websites. It is not intended to be an exhaustive listing, but includes some of our favorite resources for professionals, parents and teens.

Books for Teens on Grief and Loss

FOR THE TEENS

Death is Hard to Live With: Teenagers Talk about How to Cope with Loss
by Janet Bode, Stan Mack, Illustrator – Laurel Leaf – 1994

I just graduated from high school and feel we had a curse on my class. Six people died. The worst was Shannon, my best friend. She was free-spirited, the last person you'd expect to die. One day she's great. The next day she's dead. I wasn't prepared for it.

Facing Change – Coming Together and Falling Apart in the Teen Years
by Donna B. O'Toole – Compassion Books – 2004

A book about loss, change and possibilities, *Facing Change* is founded on the belief that young adults can make effective choices to transform pain into resiliency by understanding loss and discovering coping strategies. All kinds of losses experienced by them are recognized and validated. The author speaks to these in a straightforward, respctful and understanding way.

Healing Your Grieving Heart: 100 Practical Ideas for Teens
by Alan D. Wolfelt, Ph.D. – Companion Press – 2001

Grade 7 and up book that is written in clear, user-friendly prose. Each page presents a different idea designed to help teens recognize mourning as a natural process connected with loss, reassuring them that they should not be afraid of deep, sometimes uncontrollable emotions, and showing them how to release grief in healthy, positive ways.

When will I Stop Hurting? Teens, Loss and Grief, It Happened to Me (The Ultimate Teen Guide)
by Edward Myers – Scarecrow Press – 2004

A self-help guide for teenagers who are struggling with bereavement and the emotional difficulties ir presents. This book provides an overview of grief as a painful but normal process, and it offers insights from bereavement experts, as well as practical suggestions for coping with loss, including personal accounts from teens.

FOR THE PARENTS

Teen Grief Relief
by Heidi Horsley, Psy.D., LMSW, MS – Rainbow Books, Inc. – 2007

Help your teen grieve in a healthy way. Teenager grief is hard, lonely and painful. Parents want to know, "How can I help?" This book provides both parents and teens the help they need. Shared here are teen stories, feelings, techniques, references and resources for use in not only surviving, but thriving, after the loss of a family member or close personal friend.

FOR THE PARENTS AND PROFESSIONALS

Bereaved Children and Teens: A Support Guide for Parents and Professionals
by Earl A. Grollman (Editor) – Beacon Press – 1996

A fairly comprehensive guide to helping children and adolescents cope with the emotional, religious, social and physical aspects of a loved one's death. Topics range from how adolescents grieve differently from adults to concrete ways to help children cope.

FOR THE PROFESSIONALS

GriefWork for Teens – Whole Person Associates – 2012
by Ester A. Leutenberg and Fran Zamore, MSW, ACSW. Illustrator, Amy L. Brodsky, LISW-S

List adapted from Hospice of the Valley's Grief Speak – Books for Teens on Grief and Loss

Whole Person Associates is the leading publisher
of training resources for professionals who empower
people to create and maintain healthy lifestyles.
Our creative resources will help you work effectively with
your clients in the areas of stress management,
wellness promotion, mental health and life skills.

Please visit us at our web site: **www.wholeperson.com**.
You can check out our entire line of products,
place an order, request our print catalog, and
sign up for our monthly special notifications.

Whole Person Associates
101 West 2nd Street, Suite 203
Duluth MN 55802
800-247-6789